D0443955

DATE DUE			

George H. W. Bush

41st President of
the United States

Since the beginning of his first term as the 41st President of the United States, George Bush has faced many challenges. (David Valdez, the White House.)

George H. W. Bush
41st President of the United States

Rebecca Stefoff

 **GARRETT EDUCATIONAL CORPORATION**

Cover: *Official presidential photographic portrait of George H. W. Bush.* (The White House.)

Edited and produced by Synthegraphics Corporation

Library of Congress Cataloging in Publication Data

Stefoff, Rebecca, 1951- .
 George H. W. Bush, 41st president of the United States / Rebecca Stefoff.
    p.   cm.
 Includes bibliographical references.
 Summary: Examines the childhood, education, employment, and political career of the forty-first president.
    1. Bush, George, 1924–   . – Juvenile literature. 2. Presidents – United States – Biography – Juvenile literature. [1. Bush, George, 1924–   . 2. Presidents.] I. Title.
E882.S74   1990
973.928'092 – dc20
[B]
[92]   90-2765
ISBN 0-944483-67-4   CIP
                                             AC

Contents

Chronology for George H. W. Bush

1924 Born on June 12 at Milton, Massachusetts

1936–
1942 Attended Phillips Academy, a college preparatory school in Andover, Massachusetts

1942–
1945 Served as a pilot in the U.S. Navy during World War II

1945 Married Barbara Pierce on January 6

1945–
1948 Attended Yale University

1949–
1966 Worked as a businessman in the oil industry in Texas; became active in the state Republican Party

1967–
1970 Served in the U.S. House of Representatives

1970 Appointed U.S. ambassador to the United Nations by President Richard Nixon

1973 Became chairman of the Republican National Committee

1974 Appointed U.S. ambassador to China by President Gerald Ford

1975 Became director of the Central Intelligence Agency

1980–
1988 Served two terms as Vice-President under President Ronald Reagan

1988 Elected 41st President of the United States

Chapter 1

A Hero by Air and Sea

On December 7, 1941, a fleet of 360 fighter planes, each painted with the red rising-sun emblem of Japan, roared out of the eastern sky over the United States territory of Hawaii, in the central Pacific Ocean. Swooping in over Pearl Harbor, the U.S. naval base on the island of Oahu, the Japanese planes loosed a barrage of bombs that destroyed nearly 200 airplanes and sank or destroyed 17 American ships. They also killed or wounded 2,575 people.

When word of this surprise attack reached the U.S. mainland, Americans reacted with shock and anger. For many months, American citizens and government leaders had debated whether or not the United States should enter the great conflict that was raging in Europe and Asia — the conflict now called World War II. But the swift and deadly Japanese attack on Pearl Harbor ended all debate. Americans were now united in their desire for vengeance.

The United States promptly declared war on Japan, and American men enlisted in the armed forces by the hundreds of thousands. But none of these soldiers, sailors, marines, or airmen was more eager to serve his country in battle than a 17-year-old Massachusetts schoolboy named George Herbert Walker Bush. The day after Pearl Harbor, Bush quietly but firmly announced that he would join the Navy as soon as he graduated from school in June of 1942.

WAR IN THE PACIFIC

By the spring of 1944, George Bush was a fully qualified naval pilot — in fact, he was the youngest pilot in the U.S. Navy. Soon after completing his flight training, he was sent to the eastern Pacific Ocean, where the United States was struggling to push the once-victorious Japanese forces back toward their home islands. The struggle was a long and bloody one, as American and Japanese forces fought over every tropical island and coral reef between Hawaii and Japan.

Bush was part of the VT 51 Torpedo Bomber Squadron, which, in turn, was part of Task Force 58/38 of the Pacific Fleet. The VT 51 squadron consisted of nine TBM planes (the "TB" meant "torpedo bomber," and the "M" indicated that the planes were built by General Motors). The planes were based on an aircraft carrier called the *San Jacinto.*

Bush's job was to fly one of the planes while his two crew members, who were gunners, launched the craft's load of bombs and torpedoes at the squadron's targets. When he was back at school in Massachusetts, Bush had longed for the day when he would have a part in the war. As it turned out, he had not been in the Pacific war zone for very long before he began seeing plenty of combat action.

Attack on the Marianas

In June of 1944, the Pacific Fleet launched an all-out attack on the Mariana Islands, a cluster of about 15 small islands scattered across a wide stretch of the Pacific Ocean southeast of Japan and northeast of the Philippines. The island of Saipan, one of the largest of the Marianas, had been fortified over the years by the Japanese. Now its many landing fields and aircraft hangars provided what some people called a "stationary aircraft carrier" for fleets of Japanese fighter and bomber planes.

Saipan was designated as a U.S. target (other allied forces in the Pacific included the British, Australians, and New Zealanders). To reach it, however, American forces would have to fight their way over and around the rest of the Marianas, most of which were also well fortified with troops and anti-aircraft guns.

Task Force 58, including the VT 51 squadron, was part of the attack on the Marianas. As the fighting heated up, the pilots of the squadron, with the youthful Bush among them, waited tensely on the deck of the *San Jacinto*—or the San Jack, as they called their ship—for their orders.

Deadly TBMs

For hours, the air and sea exploded with action. The Japanese responded to the U.S. attack by sending more than 400 planes into the air in the hope of driving the American forces away. The Americans were able to shoot down about 300 of the planes, making the day a tremendous victory for the United States. But gunfire and bombs from the Japanese planes nevertheless posed a deadly threat to the San Jack.

Equally deadly as they sat on the deck of the ship were the TBMs of the VT 51 squadron, each loaded with bombs to be dropped on Japanese ships or land installations. If a bullet or bomb from the fierce fighting all around happened to strike one of the loaded TBMs, the ship and all its planes and men would be destroyed in a huge explosion. The order came down from a senior officer: the pilots must get the TBMs off the ship as soon as possible.

Unfortunately, this was easier said than done. In the thick of battle, it took nearly half an hour for the *San Jacinto* to be maneuvered into the right position for the planes to be launched. During that time, Bush sat in the cockpit of his TBM, which he called "Barbie" in honor of his fiancee, and hoped that he and the plane would make it off the deck of the San Jack in one piece.

Shot Down

Finally the ship was in position and the TBMs took off. This did not end Bush's worries, however, for he was now flying a plane filled with explosives through a hail of fire from both enemy guns and those of his own side. Within just a few moments, gunfire had damaged "Barbie's" oil system, and Bush found that he could not keep the plane aloft. He told his two crew members that they would have to ditch the plane in the ocean and abandon it.

As calmly as possible, Bush successfully piloted the TBM downward to a landing in the water. As the plane began to sink, he grabbed its life raft. The three men climbed into the raft and paddled furiously. They needed to get as far as possible from the place where "Barbie" went down because the plane had been carrying depth charges—bombs designed to be dropped at sea and to explode at certain depths underwater, damaging or destroying enemy ships and submarines.

When the sinking plane reached the depth for which the charges had been set, they would go off and the sea would explode into a mighty geyser. Fortunately for Bush and his crewmen, Leo Nadeau and John Delaney, they managed to put a safe distance between the life raft and the downed plane. The explosion, when it came, rocked them but did no damage.

Exhilarated by surviving a close brush with death, Nadeau and Delaney began to sing "Over the Bounding Main." Bush turned to them and joked, "You guys had better shut up or they're going to think we're having too good a time out here."

After only half an hour in the life raft, the three men were picked up by an American destroyer. Soon afterward, Bush was transferred to another aircraft carrier. There he was given a new TBM, and he flew this plane back to his home ship, the San Jack. Shot down at sea just weeks after reaching the Pacific combat zone, George Bush had survived a dangerous ordeal. But the war was not yet over, and worse was soon to come.

BOMBS OVER CHICHI JIMA

With American victories in the Marianas and elsewhere in the Pacific, the tide of war began to turn against the Japanese. Although Japan had been almost unstoppable in the first years of the war, 1944 saw the Americans gain control of many of Japan's Pacific island outposts. The Japanese were slowly being beaten back, with fierce fighting every step of the way, toward their own islands. And American strategy now called for attacks in Japan itself.

One barrier to such attacks was the Bonin Islands, a cluster of tiny islands located about 600 miles south of Tokyo, Japan. The Bonins were part of Japan, and the Japanese regarded them as a last line of defense for their homeland. Some of the worst fighting of the war was to take place on these tiny specks of land. One of the Bonins is Iwo Jima, where U.S. Marines would make a gallant effort in February of 1945. But George Bush was concerned with another island, one called Chichi Jima.

The Japanese operated a large radio station on Chichi Jima. There they gathered news of American bomber flights and broadcast warnings to the Japanese armed forces. As a result of these warnings, the Americans were greeted with a hail of deadly anti-aircraft fire—called "ack-ack" by the airmen—when they reached their destinations. It was clear that the Japanese radio installation on Chichi Jima had to be destroyed. The VT 51, Bush's squadron, was given the assignment.

Hit Again

On September 1, 1944 the VT 51 made a run over Chichi Jima and encountered heavy anti-aircraft fire. When the squadron tried again the next day, Bush's TBM was loaded with 500-pound bombs. Crewman Delaney was in his usual place in the rear seat, and Lieutenant William White—an officer of the squadron and a boyhood friend of Bush's—took Nadeau's place in the middle seat. They took off into a clear blue sky.

As they came over Chichi Jima, dark puffs of smoke on the ground below showed that the Japanese were once again firing ack-ack at them. As the wind tore at these warning puffs, pilot Bush spotted the radio station. He turned his TBM into a steep dive straight toward the station.

However, before Bush could complete the dive and reach

Bush was the U.S. Navy's youngest pilot during World War II. He was shot down twice over the Pacific Ocean and earned several military medals. Here he makes an equipment check in the cockpit of his torpedo bomber. (The White House.)

target distance, the TBM took a hit. The engine began to sputter, the cockpit filled with smoke, and Bush felt the plane's controls grow sluggish. He realized that the TBM was badly damaged, and he knew that he would have to abandon it soon. All he could do was try to keep it on course for a few seconds longer, in the hope that he could drop his bombs on the radio station after all.

An instant later, in spite of the dense, oily smoke that was stinging his eyes and making him choke, Bush saw that he had reached firing distance. He launched the TBM's bombs, but he could not see whether or not he had hit his target. Later, another flyer in the squadron confirmed that Bush destroyed not only the main radio building but two other buildings as well.

Bailing Out

The TBM was now burning furiously. Bush headed for the open sea, trying to give his two crewmen a chance to parachute to safety. One of the two men – no one knows whether it was White or Delaney – did manage to leave the plane, but his parachute failed to open and he was lost. Now the TBM was over the sea and out of control, only 1,000 feet above the waves. Bush pushed open the plastic canopy roof of his cockpit and leaped out.

As he left the plane, Bush was hit hard by its tail. The blow cut open his forehead, but, fortunately for him, it did not knock him out. He was still conscious moments later when he and his parachute landed in the sea. Bush was able to remove the chute before it could entangle and possibly drown him. But his second crew member was nowhere to be seen; he is believed to have gone down with the TBM.

Alone at Sea

Dazed and coughing on seawater, Bush floated helplessly. But his plight did not go unnoticed. Lieutenant Commander Donald Melvin, the commanding officer of the VT 51 squadron, had seen Bush go down. Melvin flew close overhead and, signalling to Bush through his transparent canopy, pointed to where his life raft was floating.

Bush pulled himself into the life raft and, because there were no oars, started paddling with his hands. He did not have the luxury of a few moments to relax, to gather his strength and his thoughts after the ordeal he had just been through. It was vital for him to get as far away from the island as possible, because the Japanese were already launching interception boats; they captured or killed downed Americans whenever they could. One of the VT 51 flyers swooped down over the boats, sinking several of them and turning the others back.

Bush knew, however, that the Japanese would soon be searching the area for him again. To make matters worse, the current was carrying him back toward the enemy shore. Using his hands, he paddled as furiously as be could away from Chichi Jima. But even if he escaped the Japanese, Bush knew he faced a dire fate, drifting helplessly and alone on the empty sea, without much in the way of anything to eat or drink.

The next several hours may have been among the most important in George Bush's life. Yet he has said little about them — only that his experience in the life raft forever changed his philosophy of life. But whatever he thought about as he drifted alone in the sea, his thoughts were interrupted a few hours after the crash by an unexpected but definitely most welcome sight.

THE HERO'S RESCUE

Not far from Bush's life raft, a round glass eye suddenly popped up above the surface of the sea. It was a periscope, the device used on submarines to look above the water's surface. For a few moments, Bush feared that he might have been discovered by a Japanese sub. But as the submarine continued to rise, shedding water from its rounded hull, he realized that is was an American craft. Then, to his amazement, a hatch opened and a Navy cameraman came on deck to record the rescue of the life raft and its bloodstained occupant.

The submarine was the *U.S.S. Finback*. Melvin, Bush's commanding officer, had radioed Bush's location to the American fleet, and the *Finback* was sent to pick him up. In a matter of moments, Bush was inside the officers' wardroom, where a record-player provided background music and he was given hot coffee, blankets, and medical attention for his wounded head.

A Short Leave

Bush spent the next month aboard the *Finback*, which also picked up four other stranded airmen. He learned what life was like for the crews of the "boats," as submarines were called — a tension-filled life of dodging depth charges, diving and surfacing at a moment's notice, and stalking enemy ships. He and the other flyers agreed that they preferred war in the air, with all of its hazards, to war under the sea.

Finally, Bush was brought to the naval base at Pearl Harbor. It was the bombing of this base in 1941 that had fired his desire to join the Navy in the first place. Now, in recognition of his courageous deeds, he was told he could spend a month there, resting and recovering in balmy Hawaii, where every serviceman in the Pacific dreamed of being.

But Bush was unable to relax for so long while the war still raged in the eastern Pacific. He cut his leave short. His sense of honor and duty—the same qualities that had driven him to enter the Navy back in 1942—compelled him to return to the VT 51.

With his bravery and patriotism now tested and proven under fire, Lieutenant (Junior Grade) George Bush insisted on completing his tour of duty with the squadron. It was typical of the man who would one day be President that, when he saw a job to be done, he would not shirk his responsibilities. He headed back to the San Jack.

Chapter 2

Boyhood in
New England

George Bush was born on June 12, 1924, in Milton, Massachusetts, to Prescott and Dorothy Bush. The Bushes already had one son; he had been born two years earlier. They named their first boy Prescott, Jr., after his father. The couple's second son was named George Herbert Walker Bush after his mother's father, whose name was George Herbert Walker. The story goes that Dorothy Bush wanted to name her new son after her father but could not decide which of his names to use, so she gave the boy all of his grandfather's names.

In spite of all the names he was given, young George soon acquired a nickname. His uncles—George Herbert Walker's sons—were in the habit of calling their father "Pop," so they took to calling their nephew "Little Pop." Before long, this was shortened to "Poppy." George was to carry the nickname Poppy with him all the way to the beginning of adulthood. When he grew up, he tried to lose the nickname because it sounded childish (and also because "Poppy" is sometimes used as a woman's name), but like many childhood nicknames, it proved difficult to shed.

Young George grew up with three brothers and one sister, Nancy, who is shown here with George in a picture taken soon after the Bush family moved to Greenwich, Connecticut. (The White House.)

FAMILY LIFE

The Bush family soon moved to Greenwich, Connecticut, a charming and well-to-do community on the Atlantic coast. Three more children were born to Prescott and Dorothy Bush: Nancy, a few years after George; Jonathan, in 1931; and William, who was nicknamed "Bucky," in 1938. George was especially close to his older brother, Pres. "My brothers Pres and George were thick as thieves," their sister Nancy recalled. "They were a twosome."

The two were inseparable playmates and shared a bedroom. One year their mother thought that Pres and George might like to have their own rooms, so she had a dividing wall built to make their one bedroom into two. The boys promptly asked for a special Christmas present—they wanted her to have the wall removed.

Although Pres and George had a special friendship and shared most of their activities and friends, all five of the Bush children got along well with each other. Their parents took pains to teach them certain important virtues and values: honesty, modesty, generosity. Of the five, George was especially noted for his generosity. He liked to share his toys and even his food with the others. He so often offered half of whatever he had to one of his siblings or playmates that he earned another nickname: he was called "Have Half."

School Days

The Bush children attended Greenwich Country Day School. Of course, being older than George, Pres started school earlier. Because George missed his brother and was so miserable, his father decided to let him start school a year early, even though he was small for his age.

George did well in school. In spite of his small stature,

he quickly became a leader in schoolyard games and sports. According to Pres, "George always was coordinated, even as a little guy. He had a good pair of eyes, good hands, natural reactions, and he caught and hit the ball well. He's always been quick and bright."

George was also a good student, although not an outstanding one. Teachers liked his polite manners and his friendliness. Other students liked and respected him as well. He also was not afraid or ashamed to show a sensitive, understanding side of his personality.

On one occasion, he demonstrated these qualities to a group of parents and students at an exhibition of games on Visitors' Day at school. During the obstacle race, a fat student became stuck while trying to crawl through a barrel. Most of the onlookers began to laugh, but when Dorothy Bush happened to glance at her son George, she noticed that he was crying. Without saying anything, George went out onto the playing field to help the boy out of the barrel and ran along next to him for the rest of the race.

A Church-Going Family

The Bush family belonged to the Episcopalian Church and attended services regularly. Prescott Bush's grandfather (George's great-grandfather) had been an Episcopalian minister, and the tradition of church membership and involvement in church activities was strong in the family.

Occasionally, however, as the children grew up, they received permission from their parents to play tennis instead of going to church on Sunday. Dorothy and Prescott Bush—both of whom were athletic and active—believed that healthy bodies and the ideals of good sportsmanship were important parts of a well-balanced life. They encouraged all of their children to participate in games, sports, and athletic tournaments.

SUMMERTIME IN MAINE

George Bush's childhood was not spent entirely in Greenwich. From the time he was a small boy, the Bush family spent every summer vacation in Kennebunkport, a small community on the coast of Maine. Washed by the brisk blue waves of the Atlantic and cooled by salty sea breezes, Kennebunkport was nothing more than a tiny fishing village until the early years of the 20th century. Then, it began to become popular as a summer resort for well-to-do residents of Boston, New York City, Philadelphia, and other East Coast cities.

The "summer people," as they were called by the town's year-round residents, traveled by car or train to Kennebunkport to escape the stifling heat of July and August in the big cities. Some of them rented rooms or houses, but others built their own summer homes and gradually became part of the ongoing life of the community.

Walker's Point

One of the first people to discover the pleasures of summering in Kennebunkport was David Walker, George's great-grandfather on his mother's side of the family. Together with George Herbert Walker, George's grandfather, he had purchased a big 10-bedroom house in Kennebunkport to serve as the family's vacation headquarters. The house stood on a boulder-strewn, 10-acre tongue of land that juts into the ocean. The property was known as Walker's Point.

When Dorothy Walker married Prescott Bush, her father built another, smaller house about 100 yards away from the main house for the Bushes to use. This was where George and his brothers and sister spent two lively, fun-filled, glorious months every summer. They fished, swam, played tennis, and generally enjoyed themselves with the children of other families of summer people from various East Coast cities. George has always had the ability to attract friends, and many of his friendships—even those formed during his early years—have been close and lasting ones. He is still friendly with many of the playmates from his childhood summers in Kennebunkport.

Developing Self-Confidence

The center of social and sporting life in Kennebunkport was the River Club. Most of its members were summer visitors; there was not a great deal of socializing between the summer people and the "townies," or year-round residents. In addition to a boat house, the River Club had tennis courts. Each summer, the young people would compete in tennis tournaments. George, who had become a skilled player, usually made it to the final round of the tournaments and several times took second place.

But the greatest pleasures of the Kennebunkport summers took place on the water. Swimming was not unheard of, although the Maine waters remain quite chilly even on the hottest August day, but what George really loved was boating. Grandfather Walker owned a sturdy lobster-fishing boat, and he often took the children for rides in it. When they grew a little older, he taught them how to operate the boat on their own. All of the Bush boys became good seamen, especially Pres and George. George also developed a passion for fishing. To this day, boating and fishing are among his favorite pastimes.

George's summers at Kennebunkport helped to shape the character of the man who would become President. They gave him a lifelong love of the outdoors, of physical exercise, and of recreation. His victories on the tennis court and his mastery of the lobster boat helped him build confidence in himself, although it remained a quiet confidence, never boastful. And the close-knit, family-oriented life of the summer community was very agreeable to George, who even today prefers a quiet evening spent with family members or friends to any other form of entertainment.

A FATHER'S INFLUENCE

It is likely that the single most important influence in young George Bush's life was his father, Prescott Bush, who was a most impressive and distinguished man with many accomplishments to his credit. Six feet, four inches tall, with a deep, booming voice and a mane of dark hair, Prescott Bush tended to be the center of attention in any group. He was an affectionate father, although he did not hesitate to be strict when he thought the children needed discipline.

Prescott Bush had attended a private boarding school and Yale University, just as George would do later. When George was growing up, his father worked for the investment company of Brown Brothers, Harriman in New York City; George Herbert Walker, Dorothy Bush's father, was the head of the company. He earned a substantial income, and the family lived quite comfortably, although the children were taught from an early age that it was wrong to waste money or to show off with it.

George's father was much more than a successful businessman. From an early age, George and the other children were aware of the wide range of their father's activities and achievements. They were impressed by his record in World War I. He had fought in some of the most terrible battles in France, and he had been made a captain and had received some military decorations.

The Bush children also knew that their father was a very gifted amateur singer and had belonged to many famous singing groups at Yale and afterward. He continued to be a member of private singing groups and clubs well into George's adulthood and made music an important part of the Bush family life. George was the only one of the children who never learned to sing and did not take part in the sing-alongs led by their father.

A Man Who Set Examples

Prescott Bush volunteered his time and energy for a number of church and community activities. He believed that those who are fortunate and successful have a responsibility to give something of themselves to the world around them. And he passed this belief on to his children, not by preaching but by setting an example.

George's father was a member of the Greenwich town council and the board of directors of the local hospital. During World War II, he was the head of the United Services Organization (USO), which provided recreation centers, entertainment, and other services for American soldiers and sailors around the world. In addition, he was a talented amateur athlete (he had once been a schoolboy golf champion), and he served for a time as president of the United States Golf Association.

Political Aspirations

In addition to these varied activities, Prescott Bush was involved in politics. He was a staunch Republican and often served as a fund-raiser for the Republican Party of Connecticut. He did not force his political views on his children, but all of them grew up to share his loyalty to the Republican Party.

In the late 1940s, Prescott Bush became interested in running for office. But his business partners discouraged him from seeking a seat in the U.S. House of Representatives because they felt that he was too important to their company. In the 1950s, however, he finally ran for elective office and won a seat in the U.S. Senate. Dorothy Bush, George's mother, later said that Prescott had dreams of running for the presidency. This did not happen, but it is possible that he passed along a hint of this ambition to his son George.

Prescott Bush was a U.S. senator in 1962, when this picture was taken. He was an important influence in George's life. (Copyright *Washington Post*; reprinted by permission of the D.C. Public Library.)

It is certain that George, like all the Bush children, was greatly influenced by his forceful, talented, and highly respected father. Prescott Bush was a model of clean living, hard work, and public service – a model that George Bush followed closely in his own life and career. Prescott Bush's values, advice, and assistance have guided and supported George since childhood.

AWAY TO ANDOVER

George Bush's life entered a new stage in the autumn of 1936, when he was 12 years old. Like many of the sons of well-to-do, prominent East Coast families, he was sent to a private preparatory school (also called "prep" schools, from which comes the term "preppy"). The New England prep schools are like a combination of junior high and high school. They are intended to prepare their students, who live on campus during the school year, to enter college. George was enrolled in a prep school called Phillips Academy. Because it is located on a hilltop near the city of Andover, Massachusetts, Phillips is usually called Andover.

Andover has a long and distinguished history. It was founded in 1775, one year before the start of the American Revolution. The school seal was created by the patriot and silversmith Paul Revere. At the time of George's arrival, Andover was one of the country's largest prep schools, with about 90 teachers and 900 students (all of them boys) who lived in red-brick dormitories. All in all, George must have felt that it was quite a change from living at home with his family and going to Greenwich Country Day School.

A Reputation for Fair Play

George did well at Andover from the start, both in the classrooms and on the sports fields. He was well-liked by his teachers and his fellow students, and he made many friends.

One such friend was Bruce Gelb, who arrived at Andover as a homesick, first-year student when George was one of the senior students. Some of the older boys had the habit of teasing or bullying younger students—a habit of which Bush did not approve. One day, one such bully ordered Gelb to lift and carry a heavy armchair, but Gelb could barely move it. The older boy then grabbed Gelb in a wrestling hold when suddenly an older student who had just entered the room said, "Leave the kid alone!"

The bully did not wait to argue but promptly left the scene. When Gelb asked some of the other boys who his rescuer was, they answered, "Oh, that's Poppy Bush, the finest guy in school." Says Gelb today, "At that point, he became my hero and has been ever since. Nothing makes me a more willing loyalist than a guy who sticks up for a little kid and puts a bully down. Bush has friends like me all over the U.S. and the world. The reason we stay his friends is that he is still George Bush." Bush's years at Andover gave him a reputation for fair play that has stayed with him ever since.

A Triumphant Graduation

George's prep school career was smooth sailing until he came to what was expected to be his final year. During that year he became ill with an infection in his right arm. His condition was quite serious; in fact, it could have been fatal. He had to spend a number of weeks recovering in Massachusetts General Hospital in Boston.

The infection and the long, slow recovery that followed it caused George to drop far behind in his schoolwork. His parents therefore decided that he should spend an extra year at Andover to make up for his lost classes and complete his preparations for college. Even with the extra year, however, George would still graduate with young men of his own age, because he had been a year younger than his classmates ever since his father had let him start elementary school a year early.

His final year at Andover was a time of high achievement for George. He was president of his senior class, chairman of the student deacons, captain of the baseball and soccer teams, a member of the varsity basketball team, an editor of the school paper, and more. These honors came his way because he earned them through outstanding performance and because his teachers, coaches, and fellow students recognized that he possessed great leadership ability.

A CHANGE OF PLANS

George also possessed determination and a strong will. It had been intended all along that he would enter college when he graduated from prep school. But the Japanese bombing of Pearl Harbor in December of 1941, during his final year at Andover, caused George to change his plans. He declared that he was going to enlist in the armed forces as soon as he graduated from school and passed his eighteenth birthday.

Both the graduation and the birthday came in June of 1942. The speaker at George's graduation-day ceremonies was Secretary of War Henry L. Stimson, who told the assembled young men that they should continue their educational plans and go to college. The War Department, he said, would come and get them if it needed them.

After the speech, Prescott Bush looked at George and asked if Secretary Stimson had made him change his mind. "No," George replied. "I'm going in." Prescott Bush shook his son's hand, and the way was clear for George Bush to play a hero's role in World War II.

Chapter 3
After the War

There was another person who was closely concerned with George Bush's plans at this time. This was a girl he met just a few weeks after Pearl Harbor while visiting his family during the Christmas break from Andover.

One evening, George went to a dance at the Greenwich Country Club. There his attention was captured by a smiling, brown-haired girl in a red and green dress. He persuaded a friend to introduce him to this pretty stranger, and then he asked her to dance. They danced and talked for much of the night, and by the time the evening was over, Bush knew that he wanted to see this girl again.

FALLING IN LOVE

Her name was Barbara Pierce. She was 16 years old at that time (he was 17) and attended a girls' prep school called Ashley Hall. Her family lived in Rye, New York, a suburban town not far from Greenwich.

Barbara's family was much like Bush's own family. Her father, Marvin Pierce, was the chairman of a large publishing corporation. He went into New York City to work every day, just like Prescott Bush. In addition, Barbara and her sister and two brothers went to the same kinds of schools and social events that the young Bushes attended, and they had many of the same friends. This shared background made it easy for the two young people to get to know each other quickly. They soon discovered that their feelings for one another were serious.

Bush's sister Nancy recalls that her brother was extremely popular at this time. "He was always dreamy-looking, so my friends were all crazy about coming and spending the night because of my brother," she says. "But he already was falling in love with Barbara, so their quest was in vain." Nancy describes the George Bush of the early 1940s as "sort of tall, and thin and graceful, and handsome and funny." She adds: "He was quick-witted and had a million friends."

Exchanging Family Visits

George and Barbara were very young, but they were also very sure of themselves. Although they have not discussed the details of their courtship and engagement, it is clear that they fell in love soon after their first meeting. Barbara Bush jokes that her husband never did actually propose to her, but by the summer of 1942, when Bush's military career began, their relationship was firmly established.

That summer, Barbara visited the Bush family's vacation home in Kennebunkport, and Bush spent some time with the Pierce family in Rye. Some friends of the young couple thought that they were secretly engaged. But Bush had made no secret of his deep commitment to military service, and any plans that he and Barbara might have made were for after the war.

A NAVAL AVIATOR

From the start, Bush intended to join the naval air force. The U.S. Navy required its flight trainees to have at least two years of college, but this requirement was dropped for Bush because of his excellent record and extra year at Andover. As a result, he started flight training when he was only 18 years old, and by the time he had completed the training program he was the youngest pilot in the Navy. He was and is proud of this fact, which brought him a certain amount of publicity during the war.

Flight training began at Chapel Hill, North Carolina. From there Bush was sent to flying school at Corpus Christi, Texas. The final stage of his pilot training took place closer to home, back in New England, at Charlestown, Rhode Island. He was able to get home on his leaves, and Barbara was able to visit him occasionally.

Because he was noticeably younger than the other trainees and pilots, Bush came in for a certain amount of teasing from his instructors and fellow airmen. "Even then I got the impression that my instructor thought I was still too fuzz-faced to trust with an expensive piece of Navy equipment," he remembers. His youthfulness embarrassed him a little, and he asked Barbara to tell people on the base that she was 18 years old, although she was really only 17.

War Record

After completing his training in torpedo bombers, Bush was sent to the Pacific with the VT 51 squadron. There he took part in the attacks on the Mariana Islands, when he was shot down for the first time, and also on Chichi Jima. It was while on a bombing run over Chichi Jima that he experienced the nightmare of being shot down at sea for the second time and the thrill of being rescued by the *Finback*. After this adventure, George was entitled to a long leave in Hawaii, but instead he returned to his squadron ahead of schedule.

The VT 51 squadron—with Bush at the controls of a new torpedo bomber—continued to carry out bombing raids as the Pacific war drew to a close. In all, he flew 58 missions. He is credited with having helped to sink a Japanese cargo ship near the island of Palau. Navy records also show that, during a massive attack on the Japanese-held Philippine Islands, he and a few other members of his squadron destroyed a drydock and three more cargo ships.

Official and Unofficial Recognition

For his part in the raid on Chichi Jima, Bush received the Distinguished Flying Cross. He also received three other medals for air service.

Unofficial military recognition came in the form of affection and respect from the men he worked with. The executive officer of his squadron later said that Bush "never shirked his duty and shone as the leader of the group of younger squadron men. His natural interest in people made him popular." Once again, George Bush had demonstrated that he could inspire affection and trust—qualities that would be important to his future as a political leader.

BACK TO THE STATES

Combat ended for Bush in November of 1944, when the VT 51 squadron was ordered to return to the States. But the impact of his wartime experiences has remained with him throughout his life. He faced death and saw friends die. One particularly terrible incident occurred when an American Hellcat fighter plane crashed into the deck of his ship, the *San Jacinto*. He and other crewmen watched helplessly as the plane slid into a gun mount and killed four of their shipmates.

According to Bush, this and other combat experiences

gave him vital, realistic insight into the realities of war. He has said on many occasions that the war helped prepare him for national leadership. He also believes that first-hand memories of the horrors of war are good equipment for a President because they are a strong argument in favor of peace.

Marriage to Barbara

Bush arrived home in Greenwich on Christmas Eve, December 24, 1944, just in time for the wedding of his older brother, Prescott, Jr. He followed in Pres' footsteps two weeks later, on January 6, 1945, when he and Barbara were married at her family's church in Rye.

The groom wore his Navy dress uniform, with his gold pilot's wings pinned to his chest; the bride wore a traditional white gown and veil. The wedding was a family affair: Pres was the best man, Nancy Bush was the maid of honor, and Barbara's married sister, Martha Rafferty, was the matron of honor. After the wedding, the 300 guests went to a reception at a nearby country club.

The War Ends

Despite the joyous and festive occasion, however, the country was still at war. Bush's active combat duty was over, but the Navy had other tasks for him to perform. The newlyweds enjoyed a short honeymoon at Sea Island, off the coast of Georgia, and then Bush was assigned to train young pilots at the naval air station in Norfolk, Virginia.

George and Barbara settled into the married officers' quarters on the base, where they quickly made friends with other young married couples. They were with a group of these new friends at the officers' club on the night of August 15 when they received word of Japan's surrender. Immediately, a celebration broke out, and the story goes that Bush and Barbara quietly left the party for a while to go to church.

Just weeks after returning from the war in the Pacific, Bush married his sweetheart, Barbara Pierce, in Rye, New York, on January 6, 1945. (The White House.)

By the fall of 1945, Bush had been decommissioned from the Navy and was a civilian once again. He had earned an honorable war record and had acquired valuable, although at times painful, experience. He had also started a new phase of his life by getting married. Now it was time to resume the education that he had interrupted to go to war.

YALE DAYS

Apparently there was never any doubt in George Bush's mind that he would attend Yale University, which had been his father's college. And in the fall of 1945, Yale—like most other American colleges and universities—was eager to enroll young men returning from military service. The university created a special program in which war veterans could complete the normal four years of study in just 2½ years. This program was very attractive to veterans, many of whom were married and wanted to complete their educations as soon as possible so that they could begin their careers.

Bush was one of about 8,000 freshmen who enrolled at Yale that autumn in the biggest freshman class in the university's history. Because housing was scarce in New Haven, Connecticut, where Yale is located, he and Barbara were lucky to find a small apartment.

Honors in Academics and Sports

At Yale, Bush duplicated the success in classes and sports that he had enjoyed at prep school. He won a prize for his good performance in his major, economics, and he was awarded a membership in Phi Beta Kappa, a national honor society whose members are chosen on the basis of academic excellence.

George was also recognized as one of the school's top athletes. He was a varsity soccer player, but his real love was playing first base for the baseball team. He made the varsity baseball team for three seasons in a row and was captain of the team during his senior year.

It was while Bush was captain that the team reached the finals of the National Collegiate Athletic Association's baseball championships in 1948. Five of his teammates were drafted by professional baseball clubs, and it is reported that scouts for some of the major league teams considered making an offer to Bush. If they had done so, perhaps the world would have lost a President and gained a baseball legend.

In addition to classes and sports, Bush was involved with community and public-service activities while he was at Yale. He helped raise money for the United Negro College Fund, an organization with which he continued to maintain connections after he left college. He also belonged to several private clubs, including the Delta Kappa Epsilon fraternity and the very exclusive Skull and Bones Club.

CHOOSING A CAREER

When Bush graduated from Yale in the spring of 1948, the university yearbook listed more than two dozen awards, achievements, and memberships after his name. He was clearly one of the top young men of his class.

Bush had chosen economics as his major because he intended to enter the business world as soon as he graduated from college and he wanted an understanding of the American financial system. By the time he graduated, he had even more reason to settle quickly upon a job—he had a family to support. George and Barbara Bush's first child was born in 1947, while George was still a student at Yale. They named the boy George Walker Bush.

Because of his achievements in the Navy and at college and his family's connections in the world of business, Bush did not have to go looking for a job. Instead, jobs came looking for him. His father was a member of the board of directors of Pan American Airways and had helped Prescott, Jr., get a job with that company. He offered the same assistance to George. At the same time, the firm of Brown Brothers, Harriman, where George's father remained a partner, offered the young graduate a job. But another offer turned Bush's attention in a new direction, toward the American Southwest.

Moving to Texas

That offer came from Dresser Industries, an oil-drilling company. Prescott Bush was one of Dresser's senior directors and was friendly with Neil Mallon, the company's president. In 1949, Dresser had only one trainee position available, and Mallon offered it to Bush.

The oil business looked promising to George Bush. He knew that industries of all sorts were booming now that the war was over, and that they would need fuel. Perhaps he also foresaw the huge rise in the postwar birthrate that has come to be called the "Baby Boom," which would increase the country's population and its need for fuel and energy. And perhaps he simply wanted to loosen his ties with the East Coast and strike out for new territory and a new, independent way of life, like his great-great-grandfather, who had gone west during the California gold rush a century earlier.

The job offer from Dresser Industries was Bush's chance to become involved in the latest rush for black gold in Texas. He accepted Neil Mallon's offer and headed west in his red Studebaker, with Barbara and young George set to follow as soon as he was settled. George Bush had been born and raised a New Englander, but he was about to become a Texan.

Chapter 4

Texas and Black Gold

After Bush arrived in Odessa, Texas, home of Dresser Industries, he began his first job in the oil industry. It was not a very glamorous one. Neil Mallon had arranged for Bush to fill a trainee's position in a company called Ideco, which stood for International Derrick and Equipment Company. Ideco was a division of Dresser Industries; it handled oil-drilling machinery.

In reality, Bush was something between a clerk and an odd-job man. His responsibilities included listing and cataloging machine parts, cleaning and painting equipment, and occasionally serving as a salesman in Ideco's store in Odessa. His boss, Bill Nelson, remembers that young Bush was such an energetic worker that it was sometimes hard to keep up with him. Nelson used to draw up a list every evening of chores for Bush to do the next day—only to discover in the morning that Bush had already done them all.

Within a few weeks, Barbara and little George arrived in Odessa, and the Bush family settled into the first of many houses they have occupied in Texas. This dwelling was what was called a "shotgun house," because it was long and narrow, like the box that contains a shotgun.

THE BLACK GOLD BUSINESS

During his first year at Ideco, Bush did everything from tending bar at the staff Christmas party to entertaining a visiting customer from Yugoslavia by taking him to a football game. It appears that his employers were pleased with his performance in these unusual chores as well as in his regular tasks, because before the year was out they had moved him on to the next part of his training. This was a job in Huntington Park, California, with a company called Pacific Pumps, which was also owned by Dresser Industries.

Moving Up

His job with Pacific Pumps required Bush to move his family to Bakersfield, California. He also moved up a bit, for this time he was made a salesman, selling Ideco's drilling equipment. After a short stay in Bakersfield, the Bushes lived briefly in three other California cities: Whittier (the home of future President Richard M. Nixon), Ventura, and Compton. Their second child, a girl, was born while they were living in Compton. She was named Pauline Robinson Bush but was called Robin.

As a salesman, Bush covered a wide territory. He sometimes drove as much as a thousand miles a week to reach the oil fields where his customers were sinking wells. All the while, he was acquiring firsthand knowledge of the ins and outs of the oil business, as well as meeting hundreds of people who would later be useful contacts in both his business career and in politics.

Back to Texas

Bush was transferred back to Texas after about a year in California. He did not return to Odessa, however. Instead, Dresser moved him to Midland, about 20 miles away from Odessa.

Midland was where the company's managers and sales-men lived. It was also a fast-growing community full of bright young men who were eager to become part of the oil boom. Bush was happy to be at the center of things in Midland. "Pretty soon," he recalls, "Midland was the headquarters of the independent oil men in Texas."

The independent oil men were those who owned their own small companies, and Bush decided that he wanted to be one of them. After less than three years with Dresser, he told Neil Mallon that he planned to quit and form a corpora-tion of his own with a new friend and neighbor named John Overbey. Mallon was not angry at Bush's departure and even gave the younger man valuable advice. The two remained such good friends that Bush later named one of his sons after Mallon.

BUSH-OVERBEY OIL DEVELOPMENT COMPANY

Bush and Overbey founded their new firm, Bush-Overbey Oil Development Company, Incorporated, in 1951. They received quite a bit of help from Bush's uncle, Herbert Walker, in New York City, who invested half a million dollars in Bush-Overbey. Their plans were simple. They intended to scout around for land that looked to geologists as if oil might be found under its surface. They would then either lease or buy drilling rights from the owners of the land. (Buying drilling rights meant that, in exchange for payment of a fee, Bush and Overbey would be able to drill for oil on the land and keep whatever they found.)

The entire western half of the United States was in an oil fever in the early 1950s, and the newspapers were full of stories of farmers who had struck oil in their backyards, or of wells being sunk in downtown Los Angeles. The oil business was dynamic and exciting. It offered Bush the chance to make a great deal of money if he made the right decisions and had a little good luck as well.

A Close Call

As a gold prospector, Bush's great-great-grandfather may have roamed the California hills with a pickax and a bedroll. But as an oil prospector, George spent most of his time in offices, either poring over geological survey maps or — perhaps more important — raising money from investors.

Bush did, however, have some notable adventures out in the field. One such episode took place when he and a neighbor named Gary Laughlin, an oil man who was also a pilot, flew north in Laughlin's small plane to look at a place in North Dakota where there were rumors about oil strikes. They succeeded in finding the owners of the land and making a deal, but they ran into trouble on their way back to Texas. The weather turned bad; clouds blocked their vision.

This was in the days before small private planes had sophisticated guidance instruments, so it was impossible to navigate without clear visibility. Hopelessly lost and unable to land in the thick cloud cover, Bush and Laughlin circled for hours. As they did so, ice built up on the wings and it became more and more difficult to keep the plane aloft.

Finally, though, an opening appeared in the clouds and Laughlin quickly brought the plane in for a landing. They found themselves in Miles City, Montana, off course for home but glad to be on the ground. Although both men had been pilots in World War II, both later said that this day was worse than their worst wartime flying experiences.

LIFE IN MIDLAND

At the same time that Bush was taking on the challenge of owning his own oil business, he was enjoying a comfortable, happy family life in Midland. The Bushes moved into a suburb that was popular with the oil men and their families. It consisted of many houses that were absolutely identical on the inside, so the developer who built them painted each of them a different bright color to give the community an appearance of variety. As a result, the suburb was nicknamed "Easter Egg Row." The Bushes' Easter Egg house was light blue.

George and Barbara Bush soon became part of a group of about 50 young married couples who played tennis, golf, and bridge together. Their house was a favorite gathering place, and one friend from that period remembers that Barbara never became flustered when guests dropped in. She just put some hamburgers on the grill.

Grief and Rejoicing

The early years in Midland were marred by grief and loss. At the age of three, Bush's daughter Robin became ill. A doctor diagnosed her sickness as leukemia, a type of cancer of the blood cells that often strikes children and is usually fatal.

Robin was taken to a hospital in New York City for the most advanced treatment that could be found, but in spite of all efforts, she died six months later. Some family friends have said that Barbara Bush's brown hair began to turn white at this time of sorrow. Whether this story is true or not, her hair has been white for many years.

Their grief was deeply felt, but the Bushes soon had cause for rejoicing. Three sons were born to them in Midland: John Ellis (called "Jeb") in 1954, Neil Mallon in 1955, and Marvin Pierce (named for Barbara's father) in 1956. With George Walker, this made four boys within eight years — enough to keep the Bush household lively and noisy.

Three years after Marvin's birth, the Bushes' last child, a girl, was born. She was named Dorothy, but everyone called her "Doro." The family then moved out of their Easter Egg house into a new home that Bush built. To the children's delight, it had a swimming pool.

A Popular Couple

Even while George was nursing his new business along and Barbara was raising the children, the two found time for community service. She joined a women's community-service club called the Midland Service League, and he taught Sunday school at the First Presbyterian Church. He also put his baseball skill to use and coached the Little League team.

Over time, the Bushes acquired a reputation for warmth and integrity in the Midland community. Harriet Herd, a Midland resident who knew Barbara Bush in the 1950s, says, "I have heard neighbors of the Bushes say that Barbara treated their children just like her own. They were free to come and go and play in her home and she was always there and had creative things for them to do." And Curtis Inman, a friend who was Bush's frequent badminton partner in the Midland years, remarked when Bush was elected President, "He will be the most honest person who has ever been in the White House. He is capable, and he's smart. He's everything a person wants to be."

NEW DIRECTIONS

William and Hugh Liedtke were brothers from Oklahoma who owned an independent oil exploration company. Their offices were right next door to the Bush-Overbey offices, and the four men were friends. In 1953 they merged the two companies to form a new oil company in which all of them were partners.

The four men named their new firm Zapata Petroleum, after Emiliano Zapata, a fiery Mexican revolutionary of the early 20th century. None of the men had any particular connection with Zapata, Bush later explained. They chose the name because Marlon Brando had just appeared in a popular film called *Zapata,* and they thought it would make a catchy name for their corporation.

Oil at Sea

Before long, Bush was convinced that one promising direction for the oil business was offshore oil exploration—looking for and drilling oil at sea. With the Liedtke brothers, he formed a small company called Zapata Offshore, which was a division of Zapata Petroleum that concentrated on offshore oil development. He also worked with a Mississippi-born inventor named R.G. Le Tourneau, who designed and built the world's first three-legged offshore drilling rig for Zapata.

The rig, which was nicknamed "Scorpion," cost three million dollars and weighed nine million pounds. It was towed out to sea and anchored in the seabed not far from Galveston, Texas. "Scorpion"—which might never have been constructed without Bush's faith in the inventor and his ideas—proved to be a milestone in the development of offshore drilling technology. Many three-legged rigs like it have since been built, once Zapata Offshore had demonstrated that they work.

Company President

At the end of the 1950s, Bush, Overbey, and the Liedtke brothers decided to move in separate business directions, although all four men remained friends. The Liedtkes, who were interested in the actual exploration for oil, stayed in Midland and retained control of Zapata Petroleum. Bush, how-

Bush (on the left) talks to an oil rig worker. The man who would someday become President of the United States was president of the Zapata Offshore, an oil development company, at the time. (The White House.)

ever, was more interested in renting oil rigs to other companies who wanted to explore and drill, so it was decided that he would take control of Zapata Offshore for this purpose. At about the same time, John Overbey went into new business ventures of his own.

As president of Zapata Offshore, Bush felt that the company headquarters should be in Houston, so in 1959 he moved his family into a new home there. He also relocated his staff to new offices in downtown Houston. At that time, he employed about 25 people in the main office and about 200 engineers and rig operators who worked on various drilling platforms and barges in the Gulf of Mexico.

Bush traveled widely, to the Caribbean, Mexico, and Europe, seeking out new cusomers. Many of his employees still recall how impressed they were with his energy and drive. "His name is George H. W. Bush," says Charles C. Powell, who worked for Bush in Houston, "and that H. W. stands for 'hard work,' as far as I have observed for the past 27 years!"

Bush had progressed quickly. Only a decade or so after graduating from Yale, he had become president of his own successful company. Now he was ready to move in a new direction.

POLITICAL AMBITIONS

During the 1950s, Bush had begun to dream of more than business success. C. Fred Chambers, a Midland friend, remembers an afternoon sometime in the late 1950s, before the Bushes moved to Houston, when he and George were sitting by Bush's swimming pool. Bush told his friend that he wanted to move beyond the oil business. He was interested in entering politics, he said.

Some of Bush's interest in politics at this time may have been prompted by his father's own political success. After World War II, Prescott Bush had become increasingly active in Republican Party affairs. Then, in 1950, he ran for the U.S. Senate—and lost the election by 1,000 votes.

Senator Prescott Bush

Two years later, however, a Connecticut senator died while in office and an election was held to replace him. The leading Republican candidates were Clare Booth Luce, the ambassador to Italy, and Prescott Bush. Bush won the nomination and later won the election by a healthy margin of 30,000 votes.

He took his Senate seat in 1953 (the same year that a young Massachusetts man named Jack Kennedy was sworn in as a U.S. senator) and was re-elected in 1956, this time defeating his opponent by 138,000 votes.

Prescott Bush's growing popularity with Connecticut voters may have had something to do with the fact that he was known to be a friend and golfing partner of the very well-liked President Dwight D. Eisenhower. The senior Bush served on several important Senate committees, including one that involved the huge and costly development and dam-building project known as the Tennessee Valley Authority.

Pressure from the Oil Industry

Pressure was put on Senator Bush because of his son George's connection with the oil industry. On one occasion, a group of oil men wanted a law passed that would be favorable to their interests, and they threatened to put George Bush out of business if his father did not vote in favor of the law. At other times, Prescott Bush was accused of being influenced by the oil lobby (representatives of the oil industry who worked in Washington to get senators and congressmen to vote in their favor).

Both Prescott and George Bush, however, ignored all threats and accusations. Senator Bush voted against laws that would benefit the oil industry, and his son respected his views. In fact, the two men disagreed on a number of issues that pertained to the oil industry, but they made a point of not allowing political disagreements affect their family rela-tionship.

Prescott Bush retired from the Senate in 1962 because of poor health. But George Bush was proud of his father's decade of public service — and perhaps he was inspired by his father's years in the Senate to get his own political career under way.

Chapter 5

A Rising Republican

George Bush never doubted that his future in politics lay with the Republican Party, to which he had been loyal since his school days. Texas politics, however, had been dominated by the Democratic Party for most of the past century, ever since the Civil War. Some of Bush's friends told him that if he expected to be elected to office in Texas, he would have to become a Democrat. Bush refused, saying that he was a Republican and intended to stay one. He added that he thought the time was ripe for a new surge of life in the Texas Republican organization, and he wanted to be part of it.

WORKING AT THE GRASS ROOTS

By the 1950s, Bush had much to offer the Republicans. He was clean-cut, attractive, and poised, and he knew how to present himself well to both individuals and crowds. He was the son of a distinguished U.S. senator. And he was also a war hero, a graduate of a well-known private school and one of the nation's best universities, a successful and energetic businessman, a family man, and a respected member of his church and his community.

Like many Presidents before him, Bush got his start in politics by working for his party at the local level. While he was living in Midland, he helped other local Republicans campaign for Eisenhower in 1952 and 1956. Bush's tasks no doubt included making speeches at businessmen's lunches, raising campaign contributions, getting posters printed, and the like. Such activities are sometimes called the "grass roots" of politics, because they are the foundation of the big campaigns.

FIRST CAMPAIGNS

After moving to Houston, Bush became a member of the Republican Party of Harris County, which included the city of Houston. His first position in the party came in 1962, when he was asked to join the committee that selected candidates to run for state offices. This offer suggests that the Harris County Republicans had confidence in Bush's judgment. They demonstrated that confidence again less than a year later, when the county party chairman resigned. Some members of the organization asked Bush to run for the chairman's post, which was to be filled by an election. Bush agreed. He knew that a victory in this election would be a stepping-stone to other opportunities.

First Victory

Bush's campaigning was limited to evenings and weekends, because he was still in charge of Zapata Offshore. With Barbara at his side, he spoke to dozens of clubs, groups, and meetings across the county. For her part, Barbara sat quietly and taught herself the art of needlepoint (a form of needlework similar to embroidery). She says that she had to do something to entertain herself because she could not listen to the same speech 150 times.

Bush's tireless campaigning paid off. He was elected party chairman of the county. Under his leadership, the local Republican Party attracted new members. This made the leaders of the state Republican organization look with favor upon Bush. They began to think that he had potential as a candidate for state office.

Senatorial Challenge

In 1964, one of Texas' two seats in the U.S. Senate was occupied by Ralph Yarborough, a popular Democrat who was up for re-election. The Republicans wanted to try to win the seat away from Yarborough, and some of Bush's supporters persuaded him to try for the nomination as the Republican candidate.

The first round of the contest was a victory for Bush. In the Republican primaries, he defeated Jack Cox for the nomination by winning 67 percent of the votes across the state. Now he was officially running as the Republican candidate against Yarborough.

Unfortunately for Bush, Yarborough was a far tougher opponent than Cox. President Lyndon Johnson, a Texan who had assumed the presidency when President Jack Kennedy was assassinated in November of 1963, visited Texas and campaigned in favor of Yarborough. Johnson was extremely popular in his home state, and his endorsement strengthened Yarborough's already strong position.

The Republican candidate for President, a conservative senator from Arizona named Barry Goldwater, was not well thought of by most Texans. He endorsed Bush, but his endorsement did not help the senatorial candidate. It may even have harmed his chances.

A Difficult Campaign

Bush carried on a vigorous campaign. He sought to win the votes of the black community, but southern blacks at that time traditionally voted for Democrats, and his efforts were not very successful. His campaign did not capture the loyalty or the imagination of many black voters.

The mid-1960s were a time of great racial unrest in the United States. The civil rights movement was coming of age, and blacks across the country were demanding legal and social changes to guarantee them equal rights. Many blacks felt that Bush was too conservative on the issue of civil rights — that is, he did not go far enough in making a commitment to improve the situation of black Americans. At a time when many black leaders were calling for dramatic, even violent, change, Bush stated that such change must come about through the existing system of law and political office.

Bush and his campaign committee did their best to make the candidate a public figure. They plastered the state with huge billboards reading "Bush For Senate." But because he was not widely known outside of Odessa, Midland, and Houston, many people responded by asking, "Bush who?"

Outside Help

One of Bush's allies in the campaign was the junior U.S. senator from Texas, a man named John Tower. He was a Republican who had surprised everyone by winning the Senate seat that Lyndon Johnson had given up in order to become Vice-President. Tower was the first Texas Republican to win a Senate seat since 1890. His victory in this contest was one of the things that had convinced George Bush that the Texas Republican Party was stirring with new life.

Now Tower lent his support to his fellow Republican, mentioning Bush in glowing terms in all of his speeches. (Tower and Bush became friends at this time. Years later, however, his relationship with Tower was to backfire into one of Bush's first crises as President.)

In addition to help from Tower and Goldwater, Richard Nixon, who had been Eisenhower's Vice-President for eight years, also criss-crossed Texas making speeches on Bush's behalf. He and Bush also became friendly. A few years later, when Nixon was President, he helped shape Bush's political career.

All of these efforts, however, failed to bring in enough votes. On election day, Yarborough won re-election to his Senate seat. In a statement to the *Houston Post,* Bush graciously said, "I have been trying to think whom we could blame for this and regretfully conclude that the only one I can blame is myself. I extend to Senator Ralph Yarborough, who I believe beat me fair and square, my best wishes." Bush's only satisfaction was that he had won more votes than any Republican in the history of Texas.

CONGRESSMAN BUSH

Bush has always prided himself on his ability to learn from setbacks such as his 1964 defeat for the U.S. Senate. Instead of being discouraged, he set out to do better next time.

An opportunity soon presented itself. An election was scheduled for 1966 to fill the seat in the U.S. House of Representatives from Texas' Seventh Congressional District, which included much of the middle- and upper-class sections of Houston. Confident that he could win this election, Bush declared himself a candidate in February of 1966.

Making a Commitment

But Bush had a difficult decision to make at this time. He knew that if he continued to own an oil company while running for or holding a political office, he would be accused of favoring the oil industry in legislation, as his father had been. Even if such accusations were untrue, they would cast doubt on his integrity and possibly damage his political career. He realized that he had to make a commitment to either the oil business or politics – to choose one and let the other go. He chose politics.

In 1966 Bush sold Zapata Offshore for $1.1 million. It is said that he could have made an additional $400,000, but the man who offered the higher price would not guarantee to retain all of Bush's employees. Bush therefore accepted the lower price when another buyer assured him that none of his employees would lose their jobs when he sold the company.

The Campaign of 1966

The opening speech of Bush's congressional campaign was made in Houston by former Vice-President Nixon, one of the Republican Party's top speech-makers. Bush also received help from Gerald Ford, another future President, who at that time was the Republican leader in the House of Representatives. But the lion's share of the work was done by the candidate himself.

Bush made more than 100 speeches in the Seventh District. He was sometimes accompanied by half a dozen or more young women who were called "Blue Bonnet Belles" and who handed out leaflets and brochures. Advertisements promoting Bush appeared on radio and television and in the newspapers. Posters were everywhere, and just about every resident of the district received a house call from a campaign

George and Barbara are surrounded by their five children in 1964. In that year, Bush lost his first attempt to win a U.S. Senate seat, but he was victorious two years later in a race for a seat in the U.S. House of Representatives. (The White House.)

volunteer. And the 73,000 women in the district who were registered voters received copies of a letter from Barbara Bush that included the following:

> George has a marvelous sense of humor, a great sense of being open-minded and fair. He is kind and a very hard worker, eager to learn more. All these qualities he uses to help bring up our five children.
>
> George leans heavily on his church and, in turn, serves his church. What I am trying to say is that George loves his God, his family, his friends and his fellow man.
>
> Please . . . vote with me for George!

Maybe Barbara's plea to the women voters did the trick. At any rate, this time candidate Bush was successful. The *Houston Post* reported on November 9 that he defeated his Democratic opponent, Jack Briscoe, by winning 57.6 percent of the total vote.

In the House

George was to be sworn in as a congressman in January of 1967. In the meantime, the Bushes had to move again, this time to Washington, D.C. Barbara took charge of the relocation and soon had the family settled in a large house in the northwest part of the city. The children — ranging in age from 6 to 19 — were enrolled in new schools and set about the task of making new friends and finding new activities.

Bush's first job was getting an office staff set up. He hired an office manager named Rosemary Zamaria, who describes his hectic schedule this way:

> We put in long hours to keep up with all the activity he generated, but we were happy and enjoyed our days with him. He was always so upbeat and jovial when he arrived in the morning. He would speak to everyone without fail, usually making light jokes. He was so grateful and would thank us for

every task we completed. His attendance was almost perfect, although he traveled nearly every weekend to see his Texas constituents.

In the National Spotlight

A congressman's effectiveness is determined by the committees he is appointed to in the House. Bush was lucky. He was appointed to the Ways and Means Committee, which deals with taxes and which gave him a good grounding in the nation's finances. It also offered him the chance to become something of a congressional star.

This opportunity arose when Walter Reuther, the famous and influential head of the United Automobile Workers Union (UAW), was being questioned by the committee. As a first-year congressman, Bush had to wait his turn to question the witness. That turn did not come until after 5 P.M., at which time Reuther announced importantly that he had a plane to catch.

Bush, however, insisted on taking his turn at questioning Reuther, and the committee chairman backed him up. The television cameras whirred, and those who watched that evening's news saw a determined young congressman grilling the frustrated labor leader. Texans were proud to see Bush in the national spotlight.

The Vietnam War

The late 1960s were not an easy time to be a U.S. congressman. The United States was at war in Southeast Asia, trying to keep the Communist army of North Vietnam from overcoming the weak government of South Vietnam. Like most Republicans and some Democrats, Bush supported U.S. involvement in the Vietnam War. He believed that the United

States had a duty to provide military support to a noncommunist government that wanted to prevent the Communists from taking over. Not everyone in the United States shared this view, however.

Opposition to the Vietnam War grew steadily throughout Bush's term as a congressman. Many Americans, including students on campuses across the country, came to feel that the United States had no right to interfere by force in the internal affairs of another nation—particularly since South Vietnam was not a very good example of democracy (the government there had refused to hold elections after agreeing to do so in an international conference in 1954). Protest marches and even riots between antiwar demonstrators and police became common features of American life, while both President Johnson and his successor, President Nixon, struggled to find a way to end the war.

Bush never changed his opinion that it was right for the United States to be fighting in Vietnam. He did, however, believe that American citizens, especially the young men who might be called upon to fight, deserved his personal explanation of why he felt that way. So he left instructions with his staff that he should be summoned whenever young people appeared and asked to talk about the war. Even if he was in a meeting of the Ways and Means Committee, he made time to speak to each of them.

Civil Rights

Another issue that divided the nation during this time was civil rights. Racial tension had erupted in violent riots in some American cities during the 1960s, and all politicians recognized the need to come to grips with this issue.

Although he never became an active or enthusiastic supporter of black and minority causes, Bush did come out in favor of equal rights. He voted for a law called the Fair Housing Act of 1968, which made it illegal for banks or individuals who were selling or renting housing to discriminate against minorities.

The Fair Housing Act was unpopular among conservative Texans. Nevertheless, Bush boldly went back to the Seventh District to face up to his irritated constituents. He expressed his values in a speech that ended, "Somehow it seems fundamental that a man should not have a door slammed in his face because he is a Negro or speaks with a Latin American accent. Open housing offers a ray of hope for blacks and other minorities locked out by habit and discrimination." To his surprise, he received resounding applause from an audience that might not agree with his position but could only admire his integrity.

In the summer of 1968, when Bush was running for re-election to his House seat, thousands of blacks from across the country gathered in Washington to mourn the assassination of civil-rights leader Martin Luther King, Jr. To make a dramatic gesture that would emphasize the plight of poor blacks in America, they set up a field of tents in front of the hallowed Lincoln Memorial and called it "Resurrection City" (resurrection means "rebirth"). Bush was one of many congressmen who visited "Resurrection City" to speak with black leader Ralph Abernathy, who had organized the demonstration.

Family Life in Washington

While Bush was busy fulfilling his congressional duties, Barbara Bush was dealing with the challenge of maintaining a normal family life. She was determined that the children would not suffer as a result of the move to Washington.

The Bushes continued some family traditions that they

"Resurrection City" in Washington, D.C., was a focus for political protest in 1968, during Bush's term in the House. He was one of many congressmen who visited the site of the demonstration to meet with black leaders. (Copyright *Washington Post*; reprinted by permission of the D.C. Public Library.)

had begun in Texas, such as Sunday afternoon barbecues. They also entertained neighbors, the children's playmates, and Bush's fellow congressmen and their families, often at a moment's notice. Bush had an office at home that the children were allowed to enter at any time if they wanted to see him, and he made it a point to spend time with them on weekends. They also took vacations together. During the summer, they visited Kennebunkport, where Bush had spent his own childhood summers.

SECOND SENATE RACE

As 1970 approached, Bush evaluated his political position. Twice in a row he had been elected to two-year terms in the House of Representatives, and he was pretty certain that he could be elected again. But the Republicans had taken control of the White House in 1968 when Nixon was elected President, and it seemed that this was a good time for an ambitious Republican to advance his political career.

It was generally recognized that the position of senator is somewhat more powerful than that of congressman. There are many more congressmen than there are senators, so each senator plays a larger role in the Senate than does an individual congressman in the House. Also, many political advisors feel that serving as a senator is a necessary step if one wishes some day to run for the presidency. Perhaps that thought was in Bush's mind in 1970, when he noticed that Ralph Yarborough's popularity was fading in Texas. Although his father advised him to hold on to his secure position as a congressman, Bush decided to try a second time to win Yarborough's Senate seat.

But Bush's opponent turned out not to be Yarborough after all. Another Democrat, Lloyd Bentsen, defeated Yarborough in the Democratic primary to become the party's senatorial candidate. It was Bush versus Bentsen.

Once again, Bush had the support of Senator John Tower, who claimed, "I believe Congressman George Bush would make an outstanding senator" and gave more than $72,000 in Senate Republican Party funds to Bush's campaign. Nixon also lent his support, with a strong endorsement and $100,000 from a White House election fund. (It is said that Nixon privately told Bush that if he failed to win the Senate seat he would be appointed to a high-ranking post in the Nixon administration.)

Election Blues

Bush waged his usual energetic campaign, drawing on the experience he had gained in the course of two congressional victories. He traveled a lot and used radio, television, newspapers, and house-to-house visits. And he made a point of conducting a clean campaign, discussing only issues in his speeches and making no personal attacks on Bentsen.

Bush's campaign was hurt by the fact that Barbara Jordan, who was from his home district of Houston, lent her support to Bentsen. Jordan was the first black ever elected to the Texas state senate, and she was a respected and powerful leader among the state's black population. Her support helped Bentsen win the majority of the state's black vote.

It seemed that George Bush was not destined to become a U.S. senator. On election day, Bentsen received 1,153,000 votes to Bush's 1,005,000. With his political future now uncertain, a disappointed Bush went back to Washington to serve out the remaining months of his congressional term.

Chapter 6

To China and Back

In the final months of his second congressional term, George Bush was what is called a "lame duck" congressman; that is, he was serving out the end of his term but someone else had already been elected to replace him. Traditionally, lame ducks accomplish little during their final days in office because many important tasks and decisions are reserved for their replacements.

APPOINTMENT TO THE UNITED NATIONS

Bush had one important decision to make, although it did not involve his congressional duties. President Nixon kept his pledge and offered Bush a political appointment to represent the United States at the United Nations.

Formed after World War II to serve as an international peacekeeping organization, the UN is the world center of international debate and diplomacy, where delegates, or representatives, from many nations meet in both cooperation and argument. Although it consists of many committees and sub-organizations, the two most important parts of the UN are the General Assembly and the Security Council. At its founding in 1945, the UN had 50 member nations; by 1970, membership had tripled.

Now Bush had to decide whether or not to accept the

UN post. It would give him a certain amount of prestige but very little real power or contact with the inner workings of government. On the other hand, it would allow him to remain in the world of politics, rather than returning to Texas to take up business again. It would also enable him to broaden his grasp of international affairs—something that would be necessary if he were ever to run for President. So he accepted Nixon's offer, and the appointment was announced in December of 1970.

Critics Sound Off

Bush's appointment to the United Nations post caused surprise in some circles. Many people—most of them Democrats—felt that Bush was not well qualified for the position. He had not specialized in the study of history and international affairs at school, they pointed out. Nor had he acquired the distinction, age, or experience in foreign diplomacy that were the usual qualifications for the UN post.

Perhaps the most cutting criticism came from Senator Adlai Stevenson III of Illinois, who said that Bush's appointment was "an insult" to the United States. But Bush calmly set out to prove his critics wrong, using the same combination of integrity and hard work that had helped him succeed at so many ventures in the course of his life.

At Home in New York

The appointment to the United Nations meant another move for the Bush family, this time to New York City, where the UN headquarters are located. The Bushes did not have to look for a house or apartment, however. The U.S. government maintains a residence for the family of the country's UN representative. It is a spacious set of three large interconnected

President Richard Nixon (left) meets with Bush in 1970 to discuss Bush's duties as the United States representative to the United Nations. Although some people feared that Bush was not qualified for this diplomatic post, he proved to be a hardworking and successful representative. (Copyright *Washington Post*; reprinted by permission of the D.C. Public Library.)

apartments in the famous Waldorf-Astoria Hotel on elegant Park Avenue in midtown Manhattan.

Once she had gotten the family settled, Barbara took up her responsibilities as the wife of a UN representative. She not only attended scores of diplomatic receptions and parties but also served as hostess at affairs sponsored by the U.S. delegation.

Bush, too, knew that befriending and entertaining his fellow delegates was part of his job. He threw the usual big parties expected of UN delegates, but he sometimes also took a handful of UN colleagues on less formal outings, such as to a Mets game at Shea Stadium or to Sunday dinner at his parents' house in Connecticut. He and Barbara also traveled, visiting several African and European nations on UN trips.

Bush's life was once again touched by grief during his UN years. In October of 1972, his father, Prescott Bush, died of lung cancer after a long illness. This impressive, forceful, accomplished man had given shape to Bush's character and life. Upon his father's death, Bush said that he had lost "a best friend."

THE TWO CHINAS

The two biggest challenges that Bush faced during his time as the U.S. representative at the UN involved the Communist superpowers, China and the Soviet Union. The situation involving China, in particular, was embarrassing and awkward for Bush.

At the time the UN was formed, the noncommunist government of China was headed by Chiang Kai-shek. Under his leadership, China was one of the original founding members of the UN. Later, however, a Communist movement overthrew Chiang's government, drove Chiang out of China to the small offshore island of Taiwan (also called Formosa), and renamed the country the People's Republic of China. Ever since then, Taiwan had continued to hold claim to China's seat in the General Assembly and the Security Council.

For many years, the People's Republic of China had been barred from membership in the United Nations because some countries—led by the United States—claimed that the Taiwan government was really the legal government of China. The United States did not have diplomatic relations with the People's Republic, which means that the two countries did not exchange ambassadors or in any way acknowledge each other's existence.

A Change in Position

Over time, this position began to seem less and less logical. After all, the People's Republic of China is one of the world's largest countries and has the world's largest population. People in the United States and abroad started to feel that it made no sense to keep such a vast and important country out of the UN. Each year when the China question was put to a vote in the General Assembly, it became clear that more countries favored admitting the People's Republic to the UN.

Bush, however, was one of those who felt that the United States should stand by its ally, Taiwan, and work to keep the UN from admitting the People's Republic. Thus, he was greatly surprised when, without informing him, President Nixon suddenly began sending members of his administration to Beijing, the capital of the People's Republic. It seemed clear that Nixon was bent on establishing diplomatic relations with the People's Republic, which he eventually did. In fact, Nixon visited China himself, and the opening of relations between the United States and the People's Republic of China is generally believed to have been the biggest achievement of his presidency.

Taiwan Expelled

In the meantime, Bush was caught off guard at the UN. He had urged all the delegates to vote for Taiwan and against the People's Republic – or even to vote in favor of giving UN seats to both the People's Republic and Taiwan. But in the fall of 1971, while Henry Kissinger, Nixon's national security advisor, was in Beijing, world opinion tilted strongly in favor of the People's Republic. The General Assembly voted to admit the People's Republic and to expel Taiwan (take away its UN membership).

Bush was deeply disappointed by the expulsion of Taiwan, which he regarded as America's biggest setback in the history of the UN. Nevertheless, with his typical determination to do a good and honorable job, he told his staff to be as friendly and helpful as possible to the new delegates from the People's Republic, and he made every effort to cooperate with them.

BULLETS FOR THE SOVIETS

The other major event that occurred while Bush was a UN representative was an attack on the Soviet mission, as the headquarters of the UN delegation from the Soviet Union is called. One day, while Bush was dining with members of the Belgian delegation, he received word that shots had been fired into the Soviet mission. No one was hurt; a refrigerator that had been struck by a bullet was the only casualty.

Because the incident had taken place in the United States and he was the U.S. representative to the UN, Bush hurried to the mission and promised the angry Soviets that he would make sure they were suitably protected. He kept his word and asked the mayor of New York, the city's police department, and the U.S. Secret Service to guard the Soviet mission and prevent further attacks.

Doing a Good Job

After this incident, Bush went straight to President Nixon to urge that a special task force be formed to protect foreign officials and diplomats on U.S. soil. The Executive Protection Service was created as a result of Bush's efforts.

Although critics had said that Bush was poorly qualified for his UN job, he performed very well and was generally respected. One member of the American delegation, John Stevenson, described Bush in his role as America's UN representative as "personable, very hardworking, most conscientious, and well liked by foreign delegates."

But at the end of 1972, after only two years in New York, Bush was called to Camp David, the presidential retreat in Maryland, to meet with the President. Nixon had a new job in mind for Bush.

PARTY CHAIRMAN

The Republican Party needed leadership. After Nixon was re-elected in 1972, he and other important Republicans felt that the time had come for the party to take a big step forward by adding members and winning more Senate and House seats. Nixon, who had been impressed by Bush's support on his behalf, his work as a congressman, and his efforts at the UN, now felt that Bush was just the leader that the national party needed. He asked Bush to become the chairman of the Republican National Committee.

Bush accepted the offer and took up his new job in early 1973. As always, he rolled up his shirt sleeves and got right to work. His responsibility was to oversee the operation of all the state and local Republican organizations around the country—and to make sure that party funds were wisely spent and honestly accounted for. "I'm going to miss the UN," he wrote to a friend, "but this new challenge is fantastic."

The Watergate Affair

The biggest crisis ever faced by the Republican Party took place while Bush was its national chairman. This crisis was the Watergate affair, a scandal in the Nixon administration that began when a group of over-eager Republicans broke into Democratic Party headquarters in the Watergate building in Washington in June of 1972.

Hoping to keep the matter from undermining his administration, the President told his staff members to deny that he had any knowledge of the break-in. This "cover-up," as it came to be called, was later revealed by a congressional investigating committee. The investigation into the Watergate affair also revealed a number of other unsavory facts about the Nixon White House, and criminal charges were brought against some members of the administration for tax evasion. perjury, and other crimes.

Caught in the Crossfire

The Watergate affair dragged on for more than a year, as Nixon attempted to keep his own part in the cover-up and the related scandals from becoming public. Throughout this painful period, when the nation was torn into pro-Nixon and anti-Nixon camps, Bush repeatedly found himself caught in the crossfire. On one hand, those who believed Nixon was guilty of crimes against the nation attacked the Republican Party. On the other hand, Republicans themselves were torn: some of them believed that the party should stand behind the President all the way, and some believed that the party should withdraw its support from the President so that it did not go down with him.

Bush's position as party chairman was that the party and the President are separate, and that people should not abandon the Republican Party because of the faults of one administration. His efforts helped keep the party organization together and strong.

Misplaced Loyalty

Nevertheless, many people remember that Bush spoke up in passionate support of Nixon. He defended the President in 118 speeches and 84 press conferences, claiming until the bitter end that the President had not known about the Watergate break-in or the cover-up. It was only on August 7, 1974, after Nixon's guilt was clearly established, that Bush wrote to Nixon and said, "It is my considered judgment that you should now resign."

Soon afterward, when he was on the verge of being impeached (standing trial for crimes in office), President Nixon did resign. He was the first and only U.S. President to do so. Bush, who had claimed that the President was innocent of any wrongdoing, was shown to have been quite wrong. His loyalty to Nixon may have been admirable on a personal level, like his loyalty to Taiwan, but many people felt that it was foolish and unrealistic.

AMBASSADOR TO CHINA

When Gerald Ford took over as President after Nixon's resignation, Bush hoped for a time to be chosen as Ford's Vice-President. But the choice went to Nelson Rockefeller of New York, and once again Bush was left wondering what his next step would be. Surprisingly, that next step would take him all the way to the People's Republic of China—the same country that he had tried so hard to keep out of the United Nations.

Ford offered Bush his choice of two very desirable diplomatic posts: London, England, and Paris, France. Bush turned both of them down and asked to be sent to China instead.

He felt that he would learn more about world affairs in China, and he realized that China was going to become more and more important on the international scene. His choice shows that Bush was looking ahead to his political future and thinking about what experiences would be most useful to him as a world leader.

A Light Work Load

Bush arrived in Beijing, China's capital, in 1974. For once, he had trouble finding an outlet for his energy. Because China and the United States were still in the very early stages of building a relationship, there was actually not a great deal for him to do. Meetings with important Chinese leaders were carried out by Henry Kissinger, who was now secretary of state. He visited China three times during Bush's term as ambassador. President Ford visited once as well.

As far as Bush was concerned, he dutifully arranged to have as many meetings as he could with members of the Chinese government or with cultural and business groups. He also lent his services to many of the committees, delegations, and individuals from the United States who managed to get permission from the Chinese authorities to visit Beijing.

Many Americans were eager to see China, which had been off limits to them for years. Frequently, Bush was their guide and host. One such American was Senator Charles Percy of Illinois, who said that Bush made the most of his time in China. "Bush is a curious man, and he was trying to learn everything he could," said Percy. "He was doing an extraordinarily good job early in the relationship and he helped break a lot of ice. He had a sophisticated understanding, I felt, of foreign policy."

Bush and Barbara bicycled around Beijing, the capital of the People's Republic of China, during his term as ambassador to that country in 1975. (The White House.)

Bicycling in Beijing

Because Bush's work load was not heavy, he and Barbara had plenty of time for tennis, reading, writing letters, and seeing the sights. They attended the Chinese Opera and climbed the Great Wall of China. They also became a familiar sight in Beijing, where they made a practice of pedaling around the city on bicycles, both for exercise and because they wanted to travel the way most Chinese did.

Barbara continued to practice the needlepoint skills she had taught herself years ago during Bush's first campaign in 1962 for county party chairman. She made a large rug while living in China that is now in the White House. The Bushes' children remained in the United States, either working or in school, but four of them were able to visit their parents in China. Doro, the youngest, celebrated her 16th birthday in Beijing.

Just like his UN post and his chairmanship of the Republican National Committee, Bush's tour of duty as U.S. ambassador to China was fairly brief. In November of 1975 he received a telegram summoning him back to Washington. President Ford had a new job for Bush.

HEAD OF THE CIA

The telegram was from Henry Kissinger. It read:

> The President asks that you consent to his nominating you as the new Director of the Central Intelligence Agency. . . . The President feels your appointment to be greatly in the national interest and very much hopes that you will accept. Your dedication to national service has been unremitting and I join the President in hoping that you accept this new challenge in the service of your country.

The World of Espionage

Countless books and movies have glorified the role of the spy. Real-life spies like Mata Hari, a beautiful woman who obtained military secrets from men who fell in love with her, and fictional ones like the dapper James Bond have given a glamorous, adventurous image to espionage. Yet in reality, most of the work that is done by agencies like the CIA is far less dramatic than a James Bond movie. The typical CIA agent is likely to spend much more time reading newspapers than tracking sinister enemy agents through the dark alleys of the world's most exotic cities.

The function of the CIA is intelligence-gathering. In other words, the CIA (and agencies like it in almost every country of the world) is responsible for gathering and evaluating intelligence, or information, about other countries' leaders, scientific developments, military forces, plans, and trends. Much of this intelligence is shifted and pieced together from public sources such as newspapers, radio broadcasts, and the like. It is only information that is kept secret and obtained secretly that falls into the category of espionage, or spying.

Espionage is probably as old as the existence of nations. As long ago as 400 B.C., a Chinese military expert named Sun-Tzu wrote a famous book called the *The Art of War*, in which he mentioned the importance of having reliable spies in the enemy camps. Moses is said to have sent secret agents of his own into the Holy Land to see how matters stood there. Alexander the Great had spies, as did Julius Caesar.

Under Queen Elizabeth I, during the Renaissance, England's foreign minister (equivalent to the U.S. secretary of state) had as many as 70 spies on his payroll. They brought him news of what France, Spain, and the Netherlands were doing. The French secret service was well developed also. A French agent once managed to steal a letter from the desk of one of the ministers of Queen Anne of England, and by the time Napoleon Bonaparte became emperor of France, he had an elaborate and well-organized spy network.

Espionage got its start in the United States during the Revolutionary War, when patriots spied on British troop movements. During the Civil War, the Union side had an intelligence service that was led by Allan Pinkerton, the founder of the famous Pinkerton Detective Agency.

In the 20th century, the secret intelligence-gathering services of many countries have been revolutionized by technology. Although secret agents are still irreplaceable as sources of information, much intelligence today is gathered by orbiting satellites that can take amazingly detailed pictures of foreign countries, by electronic eavesdropping devices (called ''bugs'') that can pick up a distant whisper, and by computers that create and break complicated codes in microseconds.

The largest and most sophisticated intelligence agencies today are the following: the U.S. Central Intelligence Agency, which was founded in 1947; the Soviet Union's KGB, which has secret agents both in foreign countries and within the Soviet Union; Israel's Mossad, which has concentrated on spying on terrorist groups in an attempt to put a stop to anti-Israel terrorism; and the MI-5 and MI-6 in Great Britain.

One of the most notorious spies of modern times was Harold Philby, called "Kim," an Englishman who was a secret agent for the Soviet Union. He worked for the British intelligence department from 1946 to 1951, but all the while he was giving top-secret information to the Soviets. Another was Colonel Rudolf Abel, a high-ranking Soviet spy who succeeded in operating quietly and efficiently in the United States for a number of years before being discovered and arrested in 1958.

During the 1980s, it was discovered that several U.S. embassies in foreign capitals were vulnerable to espionage. Sometimes bugs and other electronic devices were found inside them and sometimes military guards or members of the embassy staff were bribed to give secret information to enemy agents.

It seems that as long as countries are curious about each other's actions, there will always be spies—and their adventures, both real-life and fictional, will continue to fascinate the rest of us.

The Central Intelligence Agency, or CIA, is the international espionage arm of the U.S. government. It operates independently of the armed forces, although it often cooperates with them, and it is answerable to the President. The director of the CIA has three important tasks: (1) to oversee the agency to make sure that its actions are in step with the administration's foreign policy; (2) to communicate important information that is gathered by CIA agents around the world to the President or his advisors; and (3) to serve as a buffer between the highly secret agency and the public.

Bad Publicity

At the time of Bush's appointment, the CIA was suffering from a big dose of bad publicity. A Senate investigating committee had forced its previous director to make public some recent, unsuccessful CIA activities. Some Americans were shocked and angry when they learned that the CIA had attempted to assassinate foreign leaders, such as Fidel Castro of Cuba, who were considered enemies of the United States. It was also revealed that the CIA had experimented with mind-control drugs. In one tragic experiment, a CIA officer was given a drug without his knowledge or permission, and he died.

Revelations such as these made many people think that the CIA needed to be more tightly controlled by Congress. It also needed a new director to try to change its image. Bush knew that the offer of the directorship was risky. If the CIA continued to look bad to the public under his leadership, his political career might be damaged or even ended.

But Bush also knew that if he could run the agency in a fair and responsible manner that appealed to the public, it would be a major triumph. Furthermore, the CIA post was considered one of the "inside" Washington jobs, close to the President and deeply involved in high-level matters. Bush decided to accept Ford's offer. First, however, he had to be confirmed by the Senate—that is, members of a Senate committee had to vote to accept Ford's nomination of Bush for the position.

Facing the Senate

Chairman Mao Tse-Tung of China paid tribute to the efforts Bush had made while in China when he told President Ford, "We hate to see him go." Once back in Washington, Bush presented himself to the Senate committee, which was headed by his old Texas friend, John Tower.

Bush gave the committee two reasons for wanting the CIA directorship, "First," he said, "the work is desperately important to the survival of this country and to the survival of freedom around the world. Second, old-fashioned as it may seem to some, it is my duty to serve my country. And I did not seek this job but I want to do it and I will do my very best."

The Senate approved Bush's nomination, and he officially became director of the CIA in January of 1976. Ironically, President Bush would later appoint Senator Tower to a position but the nomination would be rejected by the Senate, causing the first serious setback of Bush's administration.

On the Job

The CIA headquarters are in Langley, Virginia, not far from Washington. Bush and Barbara moved back to Washington and, as he had done for most of his business and political career, Bush would work for 12 hours every day. However, the difference with this job was that because it was top-secret, he could not talk over the day's doings with Barbara when they sat down for dinner.

Bush soon discovered that running the CIA was considerably more challenging than his China post had been. Not

Senator John Tower (right) headed the Senate committee that approved Bush as director of the Central Intelligence Agency (CIA). Later, when Bush tried to make Tower his secretary of defense, the Senate refused to approve the appointment. (Copyright Washington Post; *reprinted by permission of the D.C. Public Library.)*

only did he have to learn everything about the agency and its operations, but he was kept on the go.

He met with the President once each week to summarize CIA activities. He went to the Senate or the House of Representatives almost as often in order to answer questions about what the CIA was doing. He also visited many of the agency's offices in other countries, where he took advantage of the opportunity to meet the high-ranking officers of those nations' espionage agencies. Bush admits that he never became an expert in international espionage and CIA affairs, but he surrounded himself with experts and tried to use their help wisely.

Out of a Job

Other men who have directed the CIA, including William Colby and Richard Helms, agree that Bush did a good job at the CIA. He improved the agency's tarnished public image, and he boosted morale among its employees by treating them with respect and consideration.

In turn, Bush enjoyed the job. He believed it to be important, and he found it both challenging and exciting. He has said that he would have been happy to remain CIA director for some time. But Jimmy Carter, a Democrat, was elected President in 1976.

As usually happens when the presidency shifts from one political party to the other, many jobs farther down the line of command also shift. This time, most of the Republicans who had been appointed to their posts by Republican Presidents Nixon and Ford were replaced by Carter's own selections. Bush was one of those who was replaced, after only a year at the CIA. He and Barbara returned to Houston, which they still considered their home. For the first time since he graduated from college in 1948, George Bush did not have a job.

Chapter 7

The Vice-Presidency

U pon arriving in Houston in 1977, the Bushes found that their lives had grown suddenly peaceful. Only the two youngest children—Marvin and Doro—still lived at home with their parents, and even these two went away to school for nine months of the year. Bush had no formal political responsibilities for the first time since becoming chairman of the Harris County Republican Party years before.

This was a chance for the couple to relax, to catch up on old friendships, and to plan the future. They visited China and took a boat trip up the scenic Yangtze River, through famous mountain gorges that have been celebrated in Chinese painting and poetry for hundreds of years. They also traveled to Hong Kong, Singapore, Australia, Israel, Egypt, Jordan, Iran, Greece, and Denmark.

KEEPING BUSY

But George Bush is a man who likes to keep busy. Before long, he was involved in various business ventures. He was a director and shareholder in several Texas banks and financial companies, and he returned to the oil business when he and a partner bought a number of small barges that they hired out for hauling petroleum products.

Bush also busied himself with public service. During this period, he served as a director of Baylor Medical College, as a professor at Rice University, as a trustee of his old prep school at Andover, as chairman of the American Heart Fund, and as a trustee of Trinity University. All of this activity not only kept Bush busy but also allowed him to meet many influential people and to add to his image as a thoughtful and responsible citizen. His public image was important, because he had not given up on politics. Indeed, he was ready to take a big step.

PRESIDENTIAL CAMPAIGN OF 1980

On May 1, 1979, Bush announced at the National Press Club in Washington that he intended to run for President in 1980. He ended his announcement by quoting one of President Eisenhower's speeches, in which he promised "a leadership confident of our strength, compassionate of heart, and clear in mind, as we turn to the great tasks before us." His first presidential race was under way. He kicked it off with a speech-making tour through 10 cities in New England and the South.

The first challenge Bush faced was to be nominated as the presidential candidate of the Republican Party. And he had some tough competition: Ronald Reagan, a former movie actor and governor of California, was increasingly popular with Republicans across the land. In January of 1980, a Gallup poll had bad news for Bush. It showed that Reagan was the preferred candidate of 45 percent of the registered Republican voters, while Bush was the top choice of only 6 percent.

The New Hampshire Debate

A low point in Bush's campaign was a televised debate between Reagan and Bush in Nashua, New Hampshire. Reagan, who had years of experience in front of television and movie cameras, came across to the audience as self-assured, at ease, and impressive. Bush, however, appeared nervous and irritable.

When the New Hampshire Republican Party primary was held a few days later, Reagan received 50 percent of the votes and Bush received 20 percent. Although Bush later won majorities in the Republican primaries of Massachusetts, Connecticut, Pennsylvania, and Michigan, he could never gather enough of a following to stop Reagan's progress. In the late spring, Bush finally admitted that he had no chance of being nominated. Rather than cause a split within the Republican Party by continuing to oppose Reagan, he withdrew from the race.

The Republican National Convention

The Republicans met in July in Detroit for the party's national convention. Its purpose was to nominate a presidential and vice-presidential candidate. Everyone knew the presidential candidate would be Ronald Reagan, but the number-two spot was up for grabs.

Many people expected Reagan to select former President Gerald Ford—and the voting delegates nearly always follow the choice of the presidential candidate. Bush, however, was asked to make one of the opening speeches at the convention, and the speech was warmly received by the audience. Not long after, Bush and his family and friends were waiting in their rooms at the Hotel Ponchartain. The tense silence was finally broken by the sound of a telephone ringing. Reagan had called to invite Bush to be his vice-presidential running mate. Bush's reply was swift and simple: "I'd be honored, Governor."

The Election

President Jimmy Carter, running for re-election on the Democratic ticket with Senator Walter Mondale of Minnesota as his vice-presidential candidate, did not have a chance against Reagan and Bush. Carter's presidency had been severely damaged by the hostage crisis in Iran, in which Iranian militants had seized more than 50 Americans in the U.S. embassy in Teheran and held them captive for more than a year. The country was ready for new leadership, and the Republicans won by a large margin.

In January of 1981, Ronald Reagan was sworn in as President and George Bush as Vice-President. Bush set up an office in the West Wing of the White House, not far from Reagan's own Oval Office. He and Barbara moved into a large house in northwest Washington, on the grounds of the U.S. Naval Observatory.

Surrounded by 12 acres of parklike grounds, the vice-president's house was an old-fashioned, comfortable, but elegant residence. The Bushes were to live there longer than in any of the other houses they had occupied since their marriage. They also spent as much free time as possible at the family home at Kennebunkport. Bush bought the Walker's Point estate from the rest of his family so that he could turn it into a retreat for his staff and for political friends as well as for his own children and grandchildren.

In the Oval Office of the White House, Vice-President Bush and President Reagan (left) shared weekly lunches. This one was in January of 1981, shortly before an attempt was made on Reagan's life. (National Archives.)

DUTIES OF A VICE-PRESIDENT

The official duties of the Vice-President are limited to serving as presiding officer of the Senate and standing by to fill in for the President in case of accident or illness. In reality, the Vice-President usually winds up serving on numerous committees, making a lot of speeches, and entertaining visiting officials from other countries. Bush and Reagan soon formed a close and comfortable working relationship, and Reagan frequently discussed presidential business with the Vice-President. He did not hesitate to use Bush as an assistant and a source of information.

The Shooting of the President

The new Vice-President had to cope with a crisis on March 3, 1981, just a few weeks after being inaugurated. Bush had dedicated the Old Texas Hotel in Fort Worth, Texas, as a national historic site. He was flying from Dallas to Austin in an Air Force jet when he heard shocking news: an attempt had been made to assassinate President Reagan. Bush stepped away from his aides and into a private compartment of the plane in order to pray for the President's safety.

The primary responsibility of the Vice-President, of course, is to take over the leadership of the country if the President is unable to perform his duties. Bush tried to get as much information about the situation as possible. The President had been shot by a young man named John W. Hinkley, Jr., who was later determined to be mentally disturbed. Reagan was injured and had been taken to George Washington Hospital.

That night, in Washington, Bush held a meeting of the President's advisors and Cabinet members and then calmly but firmly declared on national television: "I can reassure this nation and the watching world that the American government is functioning fully and effectively."

Bush won praise from all sides for his competent but sensitive behavior during this crisis. He showed himself to be capable of doing what had to be done, but not *too* eager to seize power. Reagan recovered completely and quickly, and he, too, gave Bush credit for his competent handling of the Cabinet, the press, and the public.

At Home and Abroad

Reagan and Bush were re-elected in 1984. Altogether, they worked as a team for a total of eight years. During that time, Bush was noted for his work in several areas, one of which was federal regulations.

Reagan had promised to reduce the amount of government red tape that businesses and individuals had to deal with, and he gave this assignment to Bush, who was chairman of

The War on Drugs

Early in his administration, President Ronald Reagan declared war on illegal drug trafficking and drug abuse. As Vice-President, Bush was expected to assist the President in the war on drugs. Reagan assigned him to do something to help improve drug law enforcement in Miami, Florida, which was where most illegal drugs were entering the country. Bush responded to this assignment by creating a unique and effective team that became the basis for new drug enforcement efforts across the nation.

The team that Bush created was called the Vice-President's South Florida Task Force. It had one specific goal: to shut down or limit the flow of illegal drugs, especially cocaine, into southern Florida. Bush brought together individuals from the federal Drug Enforcement Administration (DEA), the Coast Guard, the state and local police, the Customs Service, the FBI, the armed forces, and the Internal Revenue Service (which was good at tracing the flow of drug money and tax evasions). All of these organizations had been fighting on their own to control the drug traffic, but in the South Florida Task Force they pooled their knowledge, manpower, and skills.

The task force obtained results. Although drug trafficking continues to be a major problem in the United States in general and in South Florida in particular, Bush's task force did succeed in getting more jail space, more prosecutors and judges, and more undercover agents assigned to Miami. The task force set a new standard for cooperation among the many federal, state, and local organizations that are involved in the fight against international drug operations. Reagan later expanded it into the National Narcotics Border Interdiction System (NNBIS).

Sadly, most drug enforcement officials claim that the government still needs to devote billions of dollars more in order to stop the flow of drugs into the United States. Nevertheless, Bush's task force helped pave the way for greater efficiency in drug law enforcement, and it is regarded as one of his leading accomplishments as Vice-President.

Early in his term as President, Bush made it clear that he intended to continue the war on drugs by arresting Panamanian leader Manuel Noriega on drug-trafficking charges. He also made drug-enforcement cooperation a condition of giving financial aid to some South American countries where illegal drugs are grown and processed.

a deregulation committee for 2½ years. At the end of that time, the White House claimed that changes in federal regulations made by Bush's committee would save consumers and businesses $100 billion throughout the 1980s. These same changes would also reduce the number of work-hours devoted to government paperwork by 600 million.

Bush also promoted the use of fuels such as methanol (a form of natural gas) in order to reduce air pollution caused by ordinary gasoline. Unfortunately, this effort did not result

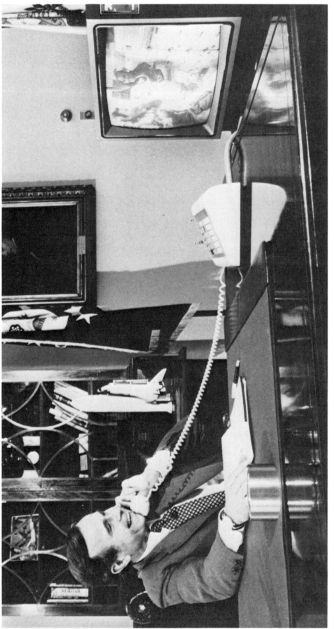

Vice-President Bush talks with astronauts John Young and Robert Crippen, who are aboard the space shuttle Columbia, while he watches them on TV. (Copyright Washington Post; reprinted by permission of the D.C. Public Library.)

in any widespread changes in Americans' gasoline consumption. But he was more successful in his ongoing determination to enact and enforce civil-rights laws to benefit disabled and handicapped people. He was regarded as a crusader for the nation's 36 million disabled citizens.

Air Force 2, the vice-presidential jet, became something of a home away from home for Bush. During his 2,677 days as Vice-President, he was away from Washington for 1,475. He visited all 50 states and 72 foreign destinations on various duties. By the end of his eight years in office, he felt that he was well-prepared to make another try for the presidency. Many Republicans—including President Reagan—agreed with him.

Chapter 8

The Campaign and the Election

As Reagan's second term as President drew to a close, many Republicans around the country were confident that their party could elect the next President. Bush, who had been Vice-President for eight years, believed that he deserved the party's presidential nomination. Once again, however, he had to face competition from other Republicans before he could try to defeat the Democrats on election day in November of 1988.

THE PARTY FAVORITE

Just as Bush had tried to beat Reagan for the nomination eight years earlier, a number of Republican politicians were eager to beat him. Foremost among them were Senator Robert Dole of Kansas, Congressman Jack Kemp of New Jersey, former governor Peter Dupont of Delaware, and Alexander Haig, former secretary of state. Pat Robertson, a minister who reached a wide audience through his religious programs on television, also ran in the primary race.

After a series of debates and primary elections in several states, it was clear that Bush was the favorite choice of the majority of Republican voters. One by one, the others dropped out of the race. By the early summer of 1988, everyone knew that Bush would be the chosen candidate when the Republican National Convention took place in New Orleans, Louisiana, in August. Now the race was on to see whom he would choose as a vice-presidential running mate.

THE IRAN-CONTRA AFFAIR

The issue that was the biggest threat to Bush's hopes of success was the same issue that rose up to cloud the final years of the Reagan administration. It was a complex web of financial dealings, deceit, and undercover operations in Latin America that has come to be called the Iran-Contra affair.

In brief, the Iran-Contra affair refers to a plan in which members of the U.S. government and military secretly sold weapons to Iran, a country with which the U.S. was on hostile terms. The money from the sale of these weapons was given to a guerrilla army in the Central American nation of Nicaragua. This guerrilla group is called the Contras (*contra* is Spanish for "against") because it is opposed to the government that took control of Nicaragua in 1979. This government is led by a group called the Sandinistas (after a Nicaraguan revolutionary hero named Sandino).

Administration Involvement

The Reagan administration supported the Contras against the Sandinistas, who are closely allied with Communist nations such as Cuba. The U.S. Congress, however, had set strict limits on the amount of military and financial help that the administration could give to the Contras. The Iran-Contra affair was basically an attempt to raise funds that could be given to the Contras without being accounted for in the usual way—in other words, it was a secret and illegal operation authorized and overseen by members of the Reagan administration.

After word of the Iran-Contra affair had leaked into the press in 1986, the House of Representatives set up a committee to investigate the matter. The case grabbed the public's attention with the much-publicized testimony of Oliver North, a Marine Corps officer who had been deeply involved in the plot. Soon people began to wonder just how much the top people in the administration had known about what was going on. Had President Reagan authorized the arms sale to Iran? Did he know about the illegal funds going to the Contras? What about Vice-President Bush?

For a long time, members of the State Department, the CIA, and the White House staff claimed that neither the President nor the Vice-President had been in on the Iran-Contra affair. Bush himself claimed that, although he knew something about the affair, he had not been involved in managing it and did not know the details. For this reason, although the Iran-Contra affair was an awkward issue during the campaign, it did not do too much damage to Bush's candidacy (in addition, many Americans did not disapprove of giving aid to the Contras). Since Bush's election, it has been shown that he knew somewhat more about the Iran-Contra affair than he admitted at the time, but there is no evidence to suggest that he authorized it or managed it.

THE CONVENTION IN NEW ORLEANS

Thousands of Republican Party delegates flocked to New Orleans in the heat of summer to select their candidates for President and Vice-President. Without hesitation, they nominated George Bush as their candidate for the presidency. Then

Bush surprised everyone by announcing his choice for a running mate: a boyish-looking 40-year-old senator from Indiana named Dan Quayle.

Almost at once, Quayle became something of an embarrassment to the Republican ticket. He was accused of having avoided participation in the Vietnam War by serving in the Indiana National Guard rather than in the armed forces. Critics also claimed that he had received poor grades in school, lacked administrative experience, knew nothing about foreign policy, and was a poor speaker. Although Quayle made a number of awkward-sounding statements and mistakes in his speeches and public appearances after being chosen by Bush, he has receded into the background of the Bush team. It is unlikely that Quayle will be as active a Vice-President under Bush as Bush was under Reagan.

Two Speeches

The morning following Bush's nomination, those who attended the convention were treated to a touching, emotional moment. A slender, white-haired man stood up on the podium in the convention center and took the microphone. No one recognized him or had any idea who he was. Then he began to speak. In a brief speech, he introduced Bush as his former World War II pilot. The speaker was Leo Nadeau, Bush's turret gunner, who had flown more than 50 missions against the Japanese with the new presidential candidate. His speech was greeted with wild applause.

That evening, Bush accepted the party's nomination in a long speech that some listeners felt was the best of his career. He talked about the achievements of the Reagan administration and said that he hoped to bring continued peace and prosperity for the future. He reminded the audience that he was in favor of such things as voluntary school prayer and

Dan Quayle, shown here in the White House garden with Bush, was Bush's choice as the vice-presidential candidate on the 1988 Republican ticket. (David Valdez, the White House.)

the death penalty for serious crimes, and that he was against abortion and increased taxes. In a phrase that has since become famous, he said, "Read my lips: no new taxes."

Bush called on Americans to clean up the environment, to improve the school systems, and to become drug-free. He wanted, he said, to usher in an era of "a kinder, gentler America." And in another phrase that lingered in the public imagination, he urged all Americans—all colors, races, and religions, from everywhere in the country—to unite and shine like "a thousand points of light."

THE ELECTION CAMPAIGN

Despite the doubts that had arisen about the choice of Dan Quayle as his running mate, Bush left the convention with the Republican Party solidly behind him. After having failed once to be nominated for the presidency and after having served eight years as Vice-President, he had finally succeeded in being nominated for President. Now all he had to do was to be elected.

Bush's Democratic opponent was Governor Michael Dukakis of Massachusetts, who had selected as his running mate Lloyd Bentsen of Texas—the same Bentsen who had defeated Bush for a seat in the U.S. Senate in 1970. Dukakis had beaten a handful of Democratic politicians to win his party's nomination. At the end of the summer, he and Bush squared off in what has been called one of the most tasteless and hollow presidential campaigns of the 20th century.

A Negative Campaign

Even Bush's supporters have admitted that very little discussion of serious issues took place during his presidential campaign. The economy, the growing cost of health care, environmental deterioration, and the possibility of an improved relationship with the Soviet Union are all subjects with which the new President would have to deal. Yet on both sides the campaign consisted mostly of attempts to make the other candidate look bad.

It seemed to many observers that neither Bush nor Dukakis had a strong, inspired vision of what he would do as President. Bush repeated his opposition to abortion and drugs and his desire to maintain a strong economy, provide jobs for everyone, and build a sound defense for America. Dukakis promised to clean up the environment and to stand up for blacks, women, and minorities. As programs, these were vague promises.

Vicious Attacks

The two sides were vicious to each other in debates. In a debate between the vice-presidential candidates, Bentsen made fun of Quayle for comparing himself to Jack Kennedy, who had been elected President at a young age. "Senator, you're no Jack Kennedy," Bentsen snapped. At a later debate, a reporter tastelessly asked Dukakis whether he would support the death penalty against a criminal who had raped and murdered his own wife, Kitty Dukakis. The entire campaign was marred by personal attacks of this nature.

Bush's hardest-hitting ads were not those that spoke about his own values but those that portrayed Dukakis in a negative way. For example, one ad reminded viewers that Dukakis had promised to clean up the environment, and then showed a picture of a pollution-filled Boston Harbor, right there in Dukakis' home state.

The most notorious ad of all, however, was an attack on the prison system in Massachusetts. In an attempt to persuade viewers that Dukakis was soft on crime, Bush's campaign ran an ad about Willie Horton, a black convicted murderer who had been sentenced to life in prison without parole in Massachusetts. While temporarily released from prison on a special furlough (a short-term leave), Horton had committed rape and murder. Bush believed that the ad would appeal to Americans who wanted strongly enforced law and order. It did, but it also raised the possibility that Bush was trying to make white voters fearful of blacks. Like many other features of both the Republican and Democratic campaigns, the Willie Horton ad was distasteful to many Americans on both sides.

ELECTION DAY 1988

In November, the campaign ended and voters marched to the polls. Bush faced the supreme test for an American politician: would he be elected President? When all the election returns had been tabulated, Bush received 54 percent of the popular vote. He also received 426 of the possible 538 votes in the electoral college. The long wait was over—George Bush was the nation's 41st President.

In his victory address, delivered before a cheering crowd in Houston on election night, Bush said, "To those who supported me, I will try to be worthy of your trust, and to those that did not, I will try to earn it, . . . my hand is out to you, . . . I want to be your President, too."

Chapter 9

President Bush

Once the election was over, Bush had two months to go before his inauguration as President—two months in which to finish out his term as Vice-President and to get ready to take on the nation's top leadership post. Many of those people who had been disappointed by what seemed like a lack of seriousness in the Bush-Dukakis campaign were impressed by how Bush set about making the necessary preparations.

In such matters as appointing people to Cabinet posts and other important positions within the new administration, Bush showed himself to be calm, thoughtful, and responsible. Above all, he showed that he intended to keep his campaign promise to respect different points of view.

A NEW STYLE IN THE WHITE HOUSE

Bush quickly showed that he wanted his administration to be one in which the President draws together information and opinions from a variety of experts and weaves the nation's policy together from these sources, rather than one in which the President single-handedly sets the nation's course. Such a "laid-back" approach is natural to Bush, who is soft-spoken and is not an aggressive or dramatic leader. But the team approach is also necessary for Bush because in the election the

Democrats had won majorities of the seats in both the Senate and the House of Representatives. This meant that Bush would have to govern with a Congress that would automatically be more opposed to him than a Congress dominated by Republicans would have been.

The practice of getting groups or individuals to agree on a course of action is called "getting a consensus," and Bush has made it clear that he will govern by consensus. In other words, his view of the presidency is that is should attempt to steer a middle ground between opposing points of view.

Bush's goal has been to promote agreement and balance among the members of his Cabinet, the Senate and House of Representatives, and the many different groups that make up the public. "I've known pretty well how I want to reach decisions," he told reporters shortly after the election. "Get good, strong, experienced people, encourage them to express their views openly, encourage them to not hold back." By balancing these views, Bush has tried to choose a cautious, practical course of action.

Relaxing a Bit

Right after the election, Bush and his family managed to snatch a few days of relaxation at the vacation house in Kennebunkport. For weeks after that, however, Bush's schedule was full from dawn until late at night as he prepared to take over the presidency.

But although he is one of the hardest-working men ever to sit in the Oval Office, Bush has always recognized the importance of exercise and rest. Therefore, he scheduled a weekend getaway for January, just before his inauguration. He went to Key West, at the southern tip of Florida, for some fishing — still one of his favorite pastimes.

*On Bush's inauguration day, more than 300,000 people stood
near the Capitol Building to see him sworn in as the 41st
President of the United States.* (Architect of the Capitol.)

Inauguration

Inauguration day was January 20, 1989. As his family looked on proudly—including his mother, who was 87 years old—George Bush stood on the steps at the west side of the Capitol Building in Washington, D.C., and was sworn in as the nation's 41st President. A crowd of 300,000 people listened as he delivered his inaugural address, a 20-minute speech in which he talked about a "new breeze" that was sweeping across the land.

Looking at the senior members of the Senate and the House of Representatives, both of whom are Democrats, Bush extended a hand in their direction and pointed out that the American people had sent him to Washington to work *with* them, not against them. Overall, his speech was about working together to solve problems—an idea that would be the main theme of the Bush presidency.

THE PRESIDENT AT WORK

Once settled in the White House, President Bush lost no time in living up to his lifelong reputation as a hard worker. His day begins early; he is often at work in the Oval Office before 7:00 A.M., either holding informal meetings with staff members or reading and writing memos.

Each morning Bush has a meeting with John Sununu, his chief of staff and right-hand man. Sununu, a former governor of New Hampshire, is one of the most important figures in the Bush administration. He arranges meetings, makes sure that the President gets necessary information, and contributes to making most decisions and plans. The morning meetings between Bush and Sununu last about an hour.

Bush also meets almost every morning with Brent Scow-

The complete Bush household consists of the President and First Lady, their children and grandchildren, and a beloved family pet. (Carol T. Powers, the White House.)

croft, the national security advisor. Scowcroft is the top official in the Bush administration where foreign relations and international affairs are concerned.

The President generally spends the afternoon reading articles, mail, and reports. Once a week he meets with the members of his Cabinet. He also greets visitors and makes and receives dozens of telephone calls; some of these conversations are with the presidents or prime ministers of other countries.

In the evening, Bush leaves the Oval Office but does not stop working. Although he and Barbara try to have dinner together every night, he spends some time each evening either doing more reading or writing notes and letters. In the morning, he gets up early to read six newspapers (or at least scan the headlines and major articles) and watch the morning news shows on television as he eats breakfast. Then he leaves for the office, carrying the correspondence he completed the night before.

Taking Time Off

This busy schedule does not leave much free time, but the President makes a point of exercising regularly, either by walking or by using a rowing machine in the White House gym. When he can, he goes to Kennebunkport for a day or two, accompanied by staff members and carrying a briefcase that bulges with work. He enjoys racing around the harbor in his speedboat, which is named *Fidelity*. He has also been known to play horseshoes on the White House lawn and to play catch with the family dogs. (Millie, the Bushes' cocker spaniel, was in the news soon after the election when she gave birth to six puppies. Photographs of Millie, the puppies, and a beaming Barbara Bush appeared in many newspapers.)

CABINET APPOINTMENTS

Bush's election was the first time that a Vice-President had been elected directly to the presidency since Vice-President Martin Van Buren succeeded Andrew Jackson as President in 1836. Because Bush had been Vice-President for eight years before becoming President, his administration was in many ways a continuation of the Reagan administration.

Bush's Cabinet—the body of people who head various government departments and advise the President on their subjects—helped smooth the transition from one administration to the next. Many of the people whom Bush appointed to serve on his Cabinet had served under Reagan as well.

Old and New Faces

Some of Bush's Cabinet members who had served under President Reagan are Elizabeth Dole, Bush's secretary of labor; Nicholas Brady, his secretary of the treasury; James A. Baker III, his secretary of state; Richard Thornburgh, his attorney general; and Clayton Yeutter, his secretary of agriculture.

Other Cabinet members include Manuel Lujan, Jr., a Hispanic-American, secretary of the interior; Jack Kemp, secretary of HUD (housing and urban development); and Louis W. Sullivan, a noted black human-rights leader, secretary of health and human services. Robert Mosbacher, a Texas oil businessman who had served as the financial officer of Bush's campaign, was named secretary of commerce and Lauro Cazavos became secretary of education. Texas Senator John Tower was selected by Bush as secretary of defense but he was not confirmed for this position. For key administrative positions, Bush appointed Richard Darman as his budget director and William J. Bennett as the director and coordinator of national drug policy.

THE EDUCATION PRESIDENT

Bush said repeatedly during his election campaign that he wanted to be remembered as "the education President." The poor quality of American school systems and the falling test scores of American students, he feels, mean that education is one of the country's biggest problems. To meet that challenge, he has vowed to put his administration's support behind the Department of Education.

Lauro Cazavos, the secretary of education, is a Hispanic-American who had served as dean of a medical school and president of a university. He shares Bush's view that the country's educational system needs a massive overhauling. He is also respected and admired; even Democrats approved of Bush's choice. Democratic Senator Ted Kennedy of Massachusetts said of Cazavos, "Clearly, this is a man who shares our views about the importance of education."

Bush and Cazavos hope to upgrade the nation's educational system by introducing such programs as cash rewards for outstanding teachers and extra funds for schools whose students' test scores improve. But only time will tell whether Bush will go down in history as the President who strengthened the country's schools.

STEPPING UP THE WAR ON DRUGS

Ever since his days as Vice-President, when he formed the South Florida Task Force to curb the drug traffic in Miami, Bush has felt that illegal drug use is one of the most serious problems facing the United States. His experience with the task force convinced him that the country stands a better chance of winning the war on drugs if the efforts of all the various law-enforcement agencies are brought together in a

Hoping to be remembered as "the education President," Bush appointed Lauro Cazavos as secretary of education and assigned him to improve the nation's public school system. (U.S. Department of Education.)

Charged with winning the war on drugs, William J. Bennett is the national director of drug policy. The position was created by Bush. (Office of National Drug Control Policy.)

single, coordinated plan. He decided that the drug problem should be a matter of national policy, just like education, commerce, and the rest of the Cabinet offices.

So Bush created a brand-new position in his administration and called it the national director of drug policy. He appointed William J. Bennett, who had been the secretary of education under President Reagan, to fill the post. Bennett was quickly given the nickname "drug czar" by the newspapers (the czar, or tsar, was the title of the emperor of Russia, and the word is now used to mean "top leader").

The President's policy on drug trafficking and illegal drug use is simple: he wants it stopped. This is a formidable task. Bennett is responsible for working with other Cabinet members, with the armed forces, and with agencies such as the Coast Guard, the FBI, and the Drug Enforcement Administration to see that every dollar budgeted for antidrug activities is spent wisely. He is also responsible for helping the President decide on new antidrug measures, such as bills to be introduced in Congress or confrontations with countries where illegal drugs are produced.

FIRST CRISIS

Bush's Cabinet appointments were widely approved by Republicans and Democrats alike. It appeared that the President had selected a capable group of advisors, with a good balance of progressive and cautious thinkers and representation from minority groups. But one appointment not only was criticized but brought about Bush's first crisis as President.

That appointment was Bush's selection of Senator John Tower of Texas as his secretary of defense. (The secretary of defense is the head of the military administration called the Pentagon and oversees all of the armed forces.) Bush and

The Ones Who Didn't Make It

The refusal of the Senate committee to approve President Bush's choice of John Tower as secretary of defense was only the eighth time in 200 years that the Senate has turned down a President's nominee for a Cabinet position.

One rejection took place in 1834, when Andrew Jackson selected Roger Taney as secretary of the treasury. It was bad luck for Taney that President Jackson was fighting bitterly with both Houses of Congress at that time over the Bank of the United States, a federal financial institution that Jackson wanted to put out of business. The Senate took out its resentment against the President by rejecting Taney.

Roger Taney's political career was not finished, however. He went on to become Chief Justice of the Supreme Court. In that position he wrote the famous ''Dred Scott decision,'' a Supreme Court ruling that defended slavery and probably helped to bring on the Civil War.

Less than a decade later, in 1843, President John Tyler nominated Caleb Cushing for the post of secretary of the treasury. Still feuding with the President over the national bank policy, the Senate said no to Cushing not once but three times—all on one day.

President Calvin Coolidge wanted a lawyer named Charles B. Warren to be his attorney general. At that time, one of the most important issues facing the attorney general was enforcing new laws against trusts (illegal alliances among companies to control the market for certain products or services). The Senate rejected Warren because they felt that he might not enforce the antitrust laws with enough energy. Warren had been a lawyer for the Sugar Trust, one of the largest and most notorious of all the trusts.

The Senate committee was overruled in the case of Henry Wallace, who was chosen by President Franklin Roosevelt to be his secretary of commerce. After the committee turned him down, Wallace went before the full Senate. He was luckier than Tower. The Senate voted in favor of his appointment, and he joined Roosevelt's Cabinet.

President Dwight Eisenhower appointed Lewis Strauss to be secretary of commerce in 1959. But Strauss had previously served as the chairman of the nation's Atomic Energy Commission. In that position, he became un-popular with the public when he ridiculed fears that atomic testing might pose health risks (fears that were later shown to be true). He also quarreled frequently with the Senate, which paid him back by refusing to confirm his appointment.

The most recent rejection before that of John Tower took place during President Rea-gan's administration. Reagan chose Robert Bork for the Supreme Court, but, in a hard-fought debate, the Senate rejected Bork be-cause it feared that he would not be fully committed to enforcing civil-rights laws.

Tower had known one another since Bush first entered politics in the 1950s, and the two men had become friends. Bush did not expect any opposition to his appointment of Tower, even though all Cabinet appointments must be approved by a committee of senators.

A Loyal President

Both Tower and Bush were stunned when the Senate committee refused to approve Tower's nomination because of widespread rumors that Tower had a drinking problem. Bush was on a whirlwind tour of Japan, China, and South Korea when he heard the news, and at once he demonstrated one of his most notable personal qualities: loyalty. He vowed to stand behind Tower and fight the Senate committee, even though his closest advisors told him that Tower was a lost cause and that he should withdraw the nomination so as not to lose the fight.

But Bush was determined not to give in. He demanded that the matter be debated by the full Senate. Unfortunately for Bush, the Senate refused to confirm Tower. The senator from Texas lost all hope of a high political office – and Bush lost his first confrontation with the Senate, which is dominated by Democrats.

Despite this setback, Bush continued to say that he intended to cooperate with the Senate and the House of Representatives. An atmosphere of cooperation was restored when the President made a second selection for secretary of defense. This nominee was Richard Cheney, a Wyoming congressman. Although he is a loyal Republican, Cheney is a capable, straightforward man who is respected by both parties. When the Senate committee swiftly confirmed Cheney's nomination, Bush's Cabinet was complete.

Chapter 10

The First Year

It is impossible to evaluate a President's successes or failures after he has been in office for only a short period of time. Indeed, sometimes many years must pass before history can judge a President. However, George Bush's first year as President was marked by some important achievements—and also by some world events that will become milestones of modern history.

EVENTS IN THE UNITED STATES

The conflict over John Tower's Cabinet nomination was the first major event of the Bush presidency. Bush weathered that storm and had his second candidate, Richard Cheney, approved by the Senate.

Just a few months later, Bush faced a new challenge when Oliver North, who had testified in Congress during the congressional investigation of the Iran-Contra affair, went on trial for criminal charges in federal court in Washington. North claimed that the Reagan administration's secret deals with the Contras were known to Bush, who was Vice-President at the time. This claim does not appear to have damaged Bush's effectiveness as President. As far as many Americans are concerned, the Iran-Contra affair is no longer front-page news. They are more interested in what the President is doing now.

Cleaner Air by 2000

One of Bush's campaign promises was to clean up the environment by passing new environmental laws and seeing to it that old laws are better enforced. Over the years, however, environmentalists have regarded the presidency as hostile to the environmental movement—or at least not very helpful to it. Therefore, environmentalists were pleasantly surprised when Bush named William Reilly as the head of the Environmental Protection Agency (EPA). Reilly, a former chairman of the World Wildlife Fund and the Conservation Foundation, is a respected environmentalist.

Bush asked Reilly to work with John Sununu and other staff members on a proposal for bringing the Clean Air Act of 1970 up to date. The consensus method was followed: several departments and agencies of the government—among them the EPA, the budget office, and the energy department—contributed information, ideas, and suggestions.

The President listened to all points of view, then sought further advice from scientists and businesspeople. Finally, he sat down with Sununu, sifted through the possibilities, and agreed to a plan that would reduce acid rain by 50 percent and smog by 40 percent by the year 2000. He announced the details of the plan on June 12, 1989. If Congress accepts this proposal and passes it into law, it will become part of the Clean Air Act.

EVENTS AROUND THE WORLD

Bush faced a diplomatic crisis during his first year in office. It involved China, the country that he had opposed admitting to the United Nations and then later served in as the U.S. ambassador.

During Bush's tour of Asia early in his term, he posed for photographers in Tienanmen Square, a huge plaza in the center of Beijing, China's capital city. He smiled and waved, with Chinese friends and representatives of the Chinese government smiling in the background. But just weeks later, news photographs of Tienanmen Square showed a very different scene.

Thousands of Chinese demonstrators, most of them young students, had jammed the square in a peaceful protest against China's Communist government. The demonstrators urged the government to enact democratic reforms, including the formation of new political parties and the holding of free elections. The smiling protestors waved posters and banners. Some of the banners showed hand-drawn pictures of the Statue of Liberty.

Tragedy in Tienanmen

The world was astonished. Although China had gradually opened itself up to Western trade and tourism during the 1980s, it had never experienced such a large and public demonstration in favor of democratic government. While television cameras and newspaper photographers from many nations captured the moment for viewers and readers everywhere, President Bush and other world leaders waited to see how China's strict Communist Party would react.

When it came, the reaction shocked and saddened Americans. After days of indecision, China's leaders ordered the army to use force to drive the demonstrators out of Tienanmen Square. Tanks, trucks, and armed soldiers moved into the square through which Bush and Barbara had bicycled so many times when he was ambassador. Gunfire broke out, and many demonstrators were killed. China's leader had shown that they were firmly opposed to the pro-democracy movement.

As a gesture of protest against the violent crushing of the demonstration, Bush immediately suspended diplomatic and trade relations with China. However, as the United Nations had realized during Bush's time at that organization, China is simply too big and too important a country for the world to ignore. By the end of the year, Bush had sent Brent Scowcroft, his national security advisor, to Beijing to begin the process of re-establishing the relationship between the United States and China.

A Helping Hand in the Philippines

Later in 1989, Bush's foreign policy was tested again, this time by events in the Philippines, an island nation in the Pacific that was once a territory of the United States. A rebel group that included Communist guerrillas and members of the armed forces tried to overthrow Corazon Aquino, the democratically elected president of the Philippines, who has been supported by the United States. This was the sixth attempt made to seize control of the Philippines from Aquino, and it was the most serious — at one time, rebel planes bombed the presidential palace.

For the first time, Aquino asked for military help from the United States. Bush answered her plea. He ordered U.S. fighter jets at Clark Air Base, a U.S. military outpost in the Philippines, to fly over the palace. The presence of the U.S. planes caused the rebel forces to back off, and Aquino was able to bring the rebellion under control.

President Bush said that there was no question that the United States would continue to support the democratic government of the Philippines. He added, however, that

Aquino needed to make changes in her administration to combat the poverty and mismanagement of government funds that are widespread in her country.

Bush and Gorbachev

One of the key figures in international events at the end of the 1980s and the beginning of the 1990s has been Mikhail Gorbachev, premier of the Soviet Union. He has introduced new attitudes and policies in the long-standing hostility between the United States and the Soviet Union, as well as within the Soviet Union itself.

As the heads of the world's two major superpowers, Bush and Gorbachev have declared that they are willing to work together to improve prospects for world peace. They began that process early in Bush's first year in the White House, when Gorbachev visited the United States. But his visit was cut short when a violent earthquake in the Soviet republic of Armenia killed thousands of people. Gorbachev flew home at once to go to the scene of the disaster.

Rough Waters at Malta

Bush and Gorbachev held a second summit meeting (as meetings between the top leaders of nations are called) in December of 1989. This meeting was held on American and Soviet ships anchored in the harbor of Malta, a small island in the Mediterranean Sea.

To the dismay of all who were there, the harbor waters were extremely rough because of a storm out at sea. The ships were tossed about, and for one whole day it was impossible to travel between the Soviet and American vessels on which the meetings were being held. At one point, however, Bush startled his staff members by venturing across the turbulent

*Soviet premier Mikhail Gorbachev (left rear) and President
Bush shake hands during the Malta summit. This meeting may
have begun an era of closer cooperation between the United
States and the Soviet Union.* (David Valdez, the White House.)

waters in a small motor launch that was almost hidden from
view by the huge waves. An experienced boater, he survived
the crossing in fine shape.

A NEW ERA

The Malta meeting was a landmark in U.S.-Soviet relations.
It was the latest in a series of summit talks on the subject
of what is usually called "the arms race"– that is, the competition by the two superpowers to equal each other's armies
and weapons. In recent years, world leaders have sought for
a way to reverse the arms race, but progress has been slow.

At Malta, President Bush offered a greater degree of
cooperation with the Soviet Union than had existed for many
years. He suggested detailed proposals for reducing the number of soldiers and missiles that each nation keeps in Europe,

and he also suggested ways that the United States could help the Soviet economy, which is in serious trouble.

Gorbachev said that he was "surprised and pleased" by Bush's willingness to meet him halfway. Although no firm decisions were made at Malta, the summit laid the foundation for closer cooperation between the two nations and for a significant cutback in the arms race. Bush and Gorbachev agreed that they would try to complete treaties on conventional weapons, nuclear weapons, and chemical weapons during 1990. And at a news conference on one of the ships, Bush became the first President in U.S. history to say that the Soviet Union—the heartland of communism—should be welcomed into the world economy.

The harmonious summit at Malta may have ushered in a new era of cooperation between the United States and the Soviet Union. If so, such cooperation will be in keeping with the enormous changes that have occurred in the Communist world since the beginning of Bush's presidency.

Changes in Europe

Under Gorbachev's leadership, the government of the Soviet Union admitted for the first time that the people of the Eastern European satellite nations have the right to choose their own form of government. (Bulgaria, East Germany, and other nations are called satellites because they have been closely controlled by the Soviet Union for many years, just as the Earth controls the orbit of the Moon, its satellite).

Within a few exciting weeks, the Berlin Wall, which had separated democratic West Berlin from Communist East Berlin since shortly after World War II, was being torn down. Communist regimes in Poland, East Germany, Romania, Czechoslovakia, Hungary, and Bulgaria were toppled from power, and new, democratic political parties were forming in those countries. The face of Europe—and the relationship between the Soviet Union and the noncommunist nations of the world—was in a process of change.

President Bush's well-timed offers of cooperation to Gorbachev have been part of the overall picture of improved relations between the two superpowers. The challenge for Bush over the rest of his term will be to see whether it is possible to trust and cooperate with a long-time enemy, and to see what results can be achieved.

OPERATION "JUST CAUSE"

Bush ended his first year in office with a dramatic gesture that silenced critics who had called him weak and indecisive. On December 20, 1989, he sent U.S. troops into Panama, in Central America, on an unheard-of mission: to arrest that country's head of state on criminal charges.

Panama's leader was General Manuel Antonio Noriega, who had been charged in a U.S. federal court with drug trafficking. He was believed to have been involved in smuggling cocaine between South America and the United States. Because of this, the Bush administration claimed that the United States had just cause (in other words, a fair reason) to launch what was really a military invasion of a country with which it was not at war. The military operation was given the code name "Just Cause."

The Elusive General

The United States built and still controls the Panama Canal and a strip of land on either side of it called the Canal Zone (the canal is due to be turned over to Panama in the year 2000). For this reason, American troops are stationed at

These U.S. Marines were part of the massive manhunt for Panamanian leader Manuel Noriega in December of 1989. Operation Just Cause was Bush's way of letting other nations know that the United States is serious about ending the international drug trade. (U.S. Department of Defense.)

several military bases in Panama. These were joined by troops flown in from the United States, until the total number of American soldiers in Panama was over 26,000.

Acting on a well-rehearsed plan, the American forces seized several air bases and other key spots, including the presidential palace, where Noriega was believed to be holed up. Almost immediately, however, the Americans realized that their quarry had escaped them. Somehow, Noriega had received word of the invasion and had slipped away from the palace.

A house-to-house search of Panama City was begun, but many people believed that Noriega had either fled the country or retreated to a hideout in the remote jungles. Meanwhile, fighting between the Americans and Noriega's armed supporters continued for several days, with casualties on both sides as well as among the civilian population.

Noriega's Downfall

Matters took a surprising turn when it was announced that Noriega had sought refuge at the residence of the papal nuncio, the representative of the Pope of the Roman Catholic Church. For several days, Noriega remained secluded with the nuncio while U.S. forces surrounded the residence to prevent the general from escaping.

Bush declared that he would not back down until Noriega either turned himself in or was handed over by the Pope. Finally, Noriega gave himself up to U.S. custody. He was flown to Florida, formally charged with breaking a variety of drug laws, and put into prison to await trial.

Bush's critics argue that Operation Just Cause was actually illegal — that it was, in fact, an armed invasion of a peaceful country. But Bush intended Operation Just Cause to be a signal to the world that the United States was going to crack down hard on the international drug trade, using military force if need be. It remains to be seen how long U.S. forces will remain in Panama, and what effect the operation will have on U.S. relations with the South American nations of Colombia, Bolivia, and Peru, all of which are sources of illegal drugs.

A GOOD START

After one year in office, George Bush had reason to feel that he was off to a good start as President. His Cabinet and staff were functioning smoothly. The Malta summit showed the world that he wanted to improve peaceful relations with the Communist bloc of nations, while Operation Just Cause showed that he could be tough when necessary.

Bush faces many challenges during the remainder of his term as President. At home, he must deal with serious problems in the economy; with homelessness, the drug crisis, and AIDS; and with education and the environment. Abroad, he must strive to follow through on the promises made at Malta and to keep the United States strong in the economic arena against competition from Asia and Europe.

One thing is certain: all his life, Bush has worked hard at whatever task he has set his hand to. He will continue to work hard for as long as he occupies the President's Oval Office. Only after his term is completed will it be possible to say how good a job he did while President.

Bibliography

Bush, George (with Victor Gold). *Looking Forward*. Garden City, New York: Doubleday, 1987. This book was put together with the help of a co-author during Bush's campaign for the presidency. It gives an account of the President's life and sets forth some of his thoughts on government.

Green, Fitzhugh. *George Bush: An Intimate Portrait*. New York: Hippocrene Books, 1989. The treatment of Bush seems rather one-sided and flattering, but this book does offer an interesting account of the President's childhood, family, Texas years, and early political career.

King, Nicholas. *George Bush: A Biography*. New York: Dodd, Mead, 1980. This campaign biography, which appeared when Bush was running for Vice-President with Ronald Reagan as the Republican presidential candidate, was designed to introduce Bush to the voters, many of whom knew nothing about the quiet politican who had served in the United Nations, China, and the Central Intelligence Agency.

Radcliffe, Donnie. *Simply Barbara Bush: A Portrait of America's Candid First Lady*. New York: Warner Books, 1989. This biography of Barbara Bush paints a flattering picture of her life with the President and their family, but it manages to capture something of her forthright, unpretentious personality and her shrewd wit.

Schneiderman, Rob. *The Picture Life of George Bush*. New York: Franklin Watts, 1989. Only 64 pages long and heavily illustrated, this book for young readers gives an overview of Bush's life from childhood through his inauguration as President.

Index

Abernathy, Ralph, 53
Andover (Phillips Academy),
    21–23, 24, 26, 77
Aquino, Corazon, 111–112

Baker, James A., III, 100
"Barbie" (fighter plane), 4
Bennett, William H., 100, 104
Bentsen, Lloyd, 55–56, 91, 92
Bonin Islands, 5–6
Brady, Nicholas, 100
Bush, Barbara Pierce (wife of
    George Herbert Walker Bush),
    24–25, 26, 28, 30, 31, 32, 33,
    38, 44, 50, 59, 68, 99
Bush, Bucky, see Bush, William
Bush, Doro, see Bush, Dorothy
Bush, Dorothy (daughter of George
    Herbert Walker Bush), 38, 68, 76
Bush, Dorothy Walker (mother of
    George Herbert Walker Bush),
    12, 14, 15, 16, 97
Bush, George Herbert Walker,
    as ambassador to China, 65–68
    as an athlete, 15, 17, 30–31, 99
    birth of, 12
    and the campaign of 1980, 77–79
    and the campaign of 1988, 88–93
    campaigns of for U.S. Senate,
        45–47, 55–56
    character of, 14–18, 21–22, 27
    childhood of, 12–18
    community service of, 38, 77
    as a congressman, 47–54, 57
    courtship of, 24–25

as director of the Central Intelli-
    gence Agency, 68, 72–75
education of, 14–15, 21–23, 30–31
entry of into politics, 41, 43–45
inauguration of, 96–97
and the Iran-Contra affair, 87–88
marriage of, 28–30
military career of, 1–11, 25–28
nicknames of, 12, 13
in oil business, 32–41
parents of, 12; see also Bush,
    Dorothy Walker, and Bush,
    Prescott
as President, 91–118
religion of, 15
as Republican Party chairman,
    63–65
as United Nations representative,
    57–63
as Vice-President, 79–91
Bush, George Walker (son of
    George Herbert Walker Bush),
    31, 32, 38
Bush, Jeb (son of George Herbert
    Walker Bush), 38
Bush, John Ellis, see Bush, Jeb
Bush, Jonathan (brother of George
    Herbert Walker Bush), 14
Bush, Marvin Pierce (son of George
    Herbert Walker Bush), 38, 76
Bush, Nancy (sister of George Her-
    bert Walker Bush), 14, 25, 28
Bush, Neil Mallon (son of George
    Herbert Walker Bush), 35, 38
Bush-Overbey Oil Development
    Company, 35–36, 38

PRESIDENTS OF THE UNITED STATES

GEORGE WASHINGTON	L. Falkof	0-944483-19-4
JOHN ADAMS	R. Stefoff	0-944483-10-0
THOMAS JEFFERSON	R. Stefoff	0-944483-07-0
JAMES MADISON	B. Polikoff	0-944483-22-4
JAMES MONROE	R. Stefoff	0-944483-11-9
JOHN QUINCY ADAMS	M. Greenblatt	0-944483-21-6
ANDREW JACKSON	R. Stefoff	0-944483-08-9
MARTIN VAN BUREN	R. Ellis	0-944483-12-7
WILLIAM HENRY HARRISON	R. Stefoff	0-944483-54-2
JOHN TYLER	L. Falkof	0-944483-60-7
JAMES K. POLK	M. Greenblatt	0-944483-04-6
ZACHARY TAYLOR	D. Collins	0-944483-17-8
MILLARD FILLMORE	K. Law	0-944483-61-5
FRANKLIN PIERCE	F. Brown	0-944483-25-9
JAMES BUCHANAN	D. Collins	0-944483-62-3
ABRAHAM LINCOLN	R. Stefoff	0-944483-14-3
ANDREW JOHNSON	R. Stevens	0-944483-16-X
ULYSSES S. GRANT	L. Falkof	0-944483-02-X
RUTHERFORD B. HAYES	N. Robbins	0-944483-23-2
JAMES A. GARFIELD	F. Brown	0-944483-63-1
CHESTER A. ARTHUR	R. Stevens	0-944483-05-4
GROVER CLEVELAND	D. Collins	0-944483-01-1
BENJAMIN HARRISON	R. Stevens	0-944483-15-1
WILLIAM McKINLEY	D. Collins	0-944483-55-0
THEODORE ROOSEVELT	R. Stefoff	0-944483-09-7
WILLIAM H. TAFT	L. Falkof	0-944483-56-9
WOODROW WILSON	D. Collins	0-944483-18-6
WARREN G. HARDING	A. Canadeo	0-944483-64-X
CALVIN COOLIDGE	R. Stevens	0-944483-57-7

HERBERT C. HOOVER	B. Polikoff	0-944483-58-5
FRANKLIN D. ROOSEVELT	M. Greenblatt	0-944483-06-2
HARRY S. TRUMAN	D. Collins	0-944483-00-3
DWIGHT D. EISENHOWER	R. Ellis	0-944483-13-5
JOHN F. KENNEDY	L. Falkof	0-944483-03-8
LYNDON B. JOHNSON	L. Falkof	0-944483-20-8
RICHARD M. NIXON	R. Stefoff	0-944483-59-3
GERALD R. FORD	D. Collins	0-944483-65-8
JAMES E. CARTER	D. Richman	0-944483-24-0
RONALD W. REAGAN	N. Robbins	0-944483-66-6
GEORGE H.W. BUSH	R. Stefoff	0-944483-67-4

GARRETT EDUCATIONAL CORPORATION
130 EAST 13TH STREET
ADA, OK 74820